the
ANSWERS

the
ANSWERS

To
Questions
That
Teachers
Most
Frequently
Ask

Julie Wofford Anderson

Skyhorse Publishing

Skyhorse Publishing books may be purchased in bulk at special discounts for sales promotion, corporate gifts, fund-raising, or educational purposes. Special editions can also be created to specifications. For details, contact the Special Sales Department, Skyhorse Publishing, 307 West 36th Street, 11th Floor, New York, NY 10018 or info@skyhorsepublishing.com.

Skyhorse® and Skyhorse Publishing® are registered trademarks of Skyhorse Publishing, Inc.®, a Delaware corporation.

Visit our website at www.skyhorsepublishing.com.

10 9 8 7 6 5 4 3 2 1

Library of Congress Cataloging-in-Publication Data is available on file.

Print ISBN: 978-1-63450-773-8
Ebook ISBN: 978-1-63450-784-4

Printed in the United States of America

CONTENTS

Acknowledgments

Thanks to Joseph Wofford and Meredith Wofford for their repeated reviews and critiques of this work as well as for their insights from a combined 50 years in education.

Many thanks also to Kenny Anderson for his repeated reviews and critiques as well as his constant support.

My appreciation also extends to Dr. Ron Cowden for reading the book and providing his insights from an administrator's point of view. Thanks also to Dr. Laura Brinker and Dr. Ed Dickey for reading the book from the perspective of teachers in training.

Finally, thanks are due to Laura Forehand who not only reviewed and critiqued the work but also provided insight into the elementary school teacher's experience.

About the Author

Julie Wofford Anderson holds Bachelor's degrees in Mathematics and Business Economics as well as a Master's degree in Educational Research. She is a certified secondary school math teacher and holds certification in supervision and evaluation. Currently a secondary math department chair and coordinator of gifted and talented programs at the high school level, as well as a math and computer science teacher, she resides in Columbia, South Carolina, with her husband, Kenny, and her daughter, Mary Elise. This is her first book.

Dedication

This book is lovingly dedicated to my husband, Kenny, and my parents, Joe and Meredith Wofford, who believed in me and my ideas. It is also dedicated to all the future teachers of my daughter, Mary Elise, in the hopes that they may teach her well and help her to become all she wants to be.

A Brief Introduction

You can already tell this book is written by a real teacher with a lot of classroom experience because the title of this section includes the word *brief*. The spare time of teachers is a precious commodity because of its extreme rarity. Therefore, I am going to be especially respectful to all teachers, new and experienced, by making this book as concise and easy to use as possible. The headings of each section are a pale attempt at humor because the ability to laugh is a requisite part of a teacher's survival during any school day. However, they are also subtitled in a rather pedestrian fashion for those who need help in a particular area in a hurry. Hence, the section with the subtitle, "Teacher Attitude," has as its main title, "It Don't Mean a Thing If It Ain't Got That Swing." Once you get into the section, you will find questions to which all teachers need answers at some point in their careers, followed by my own carefully considered answers. So you can read the book in a leisurely fashion for your personal and professional edification or in a hurry in the 4 minutes you have between classes if you need a quick answer before your fourth period class.

Finally, let me say a word about the content of this book. This is entirely a book of my responses to real questions asked by student teachers as well as first and second year teachers during the course of my counseling with them. My ideas and opinions are based on 8 years on the front lines of teaching and 3 years as an educational consultant with a state educational agency. However, I consider my main credential to be the ability to teach actual content to five classes of secondary math students the day before Christmas break without resorting to showing Christmas cartoons for the last 30 minutes of class. Seriously, I have certification in a variety of areas, including supervision of teachers, and have trained a variety of student teachers in my methods. My ideas seem to work and be helpful, so I am presenting them here for you, hoping they help you as well.

I sincerely believe that teaching is an art form that is passed from one good teacher to another through the exchange of ideas and experiences. And I am now passing along those very things to you with my sincere good wishes for a successful and enjoyable teaching career.

Julie Wofford Anderson

CHAPTER 1

IT DON'T MEAN A THING IF
IT AIN'T GOT THAT SWING

Teacher Attitude

Teaching is a professionally and personally demanding business. In addition to planning and communicating well, teachers must have style, attitude, a good sense of humor, and above all, excellent emotional health. On any given day a teacher may experience frustration, gratitude, anger, happiness, boredom, fear, exhaustion, pride, inadequacy, and impatience, often simultaneously. Often, there is no way to vent negative feelings, except perhaps in a quick stop to complain to coworkers in the faculty lounge. The experienced educator learns to suppress her feelings and smile, smile, smile. Nevertheless, these feelings are real and natural reactions to daily events, so they need to be recognized as being part of the teaching profession. Open discussion of the emotional side of teaching can lead to less stress and guilt on the part of teachers who wonder if they are the only ones who feel the way they do. This chapter is an attempt to begin that discussion.

∝∝

My students seem to have no respect for me. What can I
do to command respect?

∝∝

Unfortunately, the days when teachers automatically had respect just because they were teachers are gone. Now teachers
must both inspire and demand respect. This can be achieved
through knowing the subject matter and communicating it well,
treating students fairly, being consistent in professional judg-
ments and actions, and acknowledging when you are wrong.
However, the fact that you possess all these great qualities will
remain forever unknown to your classes unless you can get them
quiet and still long enough to demonstrate your excellence.
Some ways to quickly project an image of extreme confidence,
and thereby gain the initial respect needed, are the following:

- Speak in a firm, clear voice.

- Do not talk over students' voices. Respect yourself enough
  to believe that what you have to say is important and
  deserves to be heard. (See the section on discipline for
  ideas on how to get students quiet enough to listen.)

- At the beginning of class, briefly state what you intend to
  do and the order in which you are going to do it. This lets
  the students know that you are in charge and that you
  have a plan as well as expectations of their participation.
  Structure is necessary for all students and is especially
  important for elementary and middle school students.

- Move around the classroom. Nothing lets students know
  that you are intimidated more than standing behind a
  lectern or desk.

- Be alert to disciplinary problems and take action fairly and immediately.

- Do not tolerate misbehavior from students. Take whatever action is appropriate, and whatever you do, do not grin and bear it. You will appear ineffectual.

- Show respect for students and do not tolerate disrespect toward yourself or other students. Modeling is always one of the best ways of teaching.

- Do all things consistently so that students know that you say what you mean and you mean what you say.

I have a student who thinks I don't like her. What can I do to make her understand I like her?

First of all, get a reality check. You are not there for students to like; you are there to be their teacher. They are the *children* and you are the *adult*! Teachers are so isolated from adult company during the day that they begin to think of their students as their peers, but they are not! If you are a secondary teacher and students complain that you do not like them, simply tell them that you do not know them well enough to judge whether you like them or not. Also tell the students that your opinion of them is based solely on their behavior in your class for the few hours you see them each week, so if they want a good opinion from the teacher, they should behave appropriately. If you are an elementary teacher, you are in a position of spending all day with the child and you do know them fairly well, so this line of reasoning will not work for you. Elementary teachers as well as secondary teachers know that there are some students they may not like as well as others. Both types of teachers might benefit from a quick personal inventory of whether they are sending negative messages in some way toward a student. If you are truthful and find that you have been doing this, you need to provide some positive reinforcement for that child each time you see him or her. If you really find no fault with your own behavior, let the matter drop and do not dwell on it during class time *or* your personal time. Some students will like you and some will not; that is life.

The classes I am teaching are so remedial. I am incredibly bored by the material as well as by the fact that I have to continually repeat basic concepts over and over again. How can I keep from dying of boredom?

This feeling of boredom is common not only when teaching remedial courses but also in the cases of teachers who have taught the same subject or grade level for so many years that they can teach the class on autopilot and can anticipate student questions before they are even asked. The nice thing about teaching, however, is that you really are in control of your workday. You do not have to be bored if you choose to do interesting things with your students and your material. Try some new ideas such as integrating technology and new software into your classes, taking your classes on field trips (even if it is just around the school to do projects), or integrating your lessons with other teachers from different disciplines (e.g., blending a class in basic geometry with the art teacher's lessons on shapes). If you are bored by your lessons, it is a sure bet that your students are as well. You have the power to make your day, as well as your students' day, interesting. Also, do not forget that although the material may be old to you, it is new to your students.

I feel as if I am drowning under mountains of work! There is so much to be done! There are so many details and so little time in the workday to do the work because I have to be teaching or helping students all day! I end up working all night and I am absolutely exhausted and stressed to the maximum! Help!

First of all, take a deep breath and realize that you are talking only about your job, not your entire life. Your problem is that your job has consumed your life at this point. You have got to get some balance. Let us tackle the "mountains of work" problem. Who is making this mountain? Although some of it may be imposed by the administration, what about the majority of it? If you are like most teachers, chances are that the majority of the work is of your making, so unmake it! You might want to take a look at the section in this book on organization that discusses planning with yourself, as well as your students, in mind. You will not be a good teacher if you are harried, frazzled, and exhausted, and you will not be inclined to stick with this occupation for very long either. Promise yourself that you will not work on school-related matters on the weekend, and once you have mastered that, promise yourself that you will not work after 5 p.m. Eventually, you will find that you can plan your work in such a way that will get it all done in a reasonable time period, and the extraneous work that is consuming you now will fall away.

I have always prided myself on having a very even temper, but my students seem to be deliberately trying to upset me! I yell at them and I have actually thrown things on the floor! This, of course, seems to delight them, which makes me even madder! I am really becoming afraid that I might do something stupid in the heat of the moment that will cost me my job. How can I keep my cool?

Students can really push a teacher's buttons. Part of the reason for this is that some teachers tend to interpret the abuse they encounter as personal attacks. One of the hardest tactics to learn as a teacher is to keep yourself and your personal feelings shielded and out of the picture. Even if you or your family members really are being personally attacked, you need to simply act in a calm and detached manner that shows the students they are not getting to you. By all means, take disciplinary action that is appropriate and do so consistently. Once they realize that they will suffer unpleasant consequences as well as be deprived of the joy of seeing you upset, they will simply stop trying to get your goat. This will give a great outward appearance, but how do you deal with the raging inferno of anger inside of yourself? Simply say to yourself that these are children, whether they are 18 years old and 6 feet tall or 6 years old and 4 feet tall, and children should never be masters over an adult's feelings. By reacting to their behavior in a hysterical fashion, you are playing into their hands and letting them dictate what your behavior should be. Once you look at the situation this way, it is much easier to detach yourself from it and behave in a professional manner. Try it and see if it does not become much easier with practice. If you stay in teaching, you should have plenty of practice!

After I have explained or demonstrated some concept for what seems like the millionth time, it still seems like I am not getting through to my students. When they do badly on quizzes, I feel even more inadequate as a teacher. I am so frustrated at their inability to learn. Is it just that they are not trying hard? I feel as if I am trying to force knowledge on them and they are resisting with all their might.

Accept the fact that some students really are resisting learning with all their might. For whatever reasons, at different stages in their development, some students rebel against all common sense and do to themselves the worst possible things in all areas of their lives. Your job is to keep plugging away every day in the hopes that some of the knowledge you are trying to impart reaches them. Remember also that not all of your students are in this difficult stage of development at the same time, so you are getting through to some of them. If you really are not getting through to the majority of your students and this is demonstrated by their poor performances on quizzes, you need to take some action. Any professional knows to try something different when the status quo no longer works. Try asking a teacher or an administrator whose opinions you value to observe your classes and offer ideas to help you reach your students. There are many seminars and courses offered by districts and universities that deal with techniques for motivating students and teaching to different learning styles. Finally, try asking your students through class discussions or surveys what they feel would help them learn best. You will usually get some really good responses from your students that will actually help improve your instruction. Do not get discouraged. If your first attempts at change do not work, keep trying. Eventually, something you do will make a huge difference.

Lately, I find myself losing patience frequently throughout the day. It seems like I have heard all the excuses, lame comments, and general silliness from students one time too many. When they do not understand a concept after what I felt was a reasonable period of instruction, I lose it and basically think, "What's the point?" My impatience has extended to the administration as well, and I find myself being extremely sarcastic when faced with what I believe to be yet another inane requirement forced on me. How can I control this growing sense of having a very short fuse?

This is a very common feeling among teachers, and it is not without reason. You most likely *have* heard it all before, and frankly it is somewhat tiresome. Is spring break or Christmas break coming up? Use this time to completely break free of any-thing related to school and give yourself a chance to refresh. If no breaks are in sight, take a personal day and go off on a 3-day weekend. At the very least, plan an activity you can happily anticipate that is not school related, such as taking up hobbies or reading only books that are for pleasure. In short, focus on things that make you happy. Remember that there is a certain comfort to be derived from the familiar, and it sounds like you are squarely planted in familiar ground each workday. When students confront you with the same old song and dance, change your reaction. Make a joke, be dramatic and pretend to faint, or do whatever it takes to make your day a little more interesting. When administrators present you with what you feel is inane work, turn it to your advantage. After all, you are a professional with a lot of knowledge, so show it off to those administrators and blow your own horn for a change. Patience is not only a virtue but also how you survive as a teacher. So do whatever it takes to cultivate it in yourself, and pretty soon you will find it is with you almost all the time.

I am a new teacher and I feel intimidated by teachers who have been around for a while as well as by the administrators. They all seem to know so much and be so much more efficient than I am. I am afraid to voice an opinion because I might look as stupid as I feel sometimes. I feel I could use their help, but again, I am too intimidated to ask for it. What if they see how much I need to learn about teaching and decide to fire me because I am not yet tenured?

Everybody you are referring to was once in your place. If you ask them, most of them also remember the feelings of being intimidated. There is a lot to learn about teaching, and who better to learn from than those who have done it? Many school districts have a planned mentoring program that pairs experienced teachers with new teachers to help provide on-the-job training in a nonjudgmental way. If your district does not have this, you will still find that more experienced teachers are an invaluable resource. Find teachers that you seem to click with the most and enlist their help with your problems. Ask them to come watch your classes, or go watch theirs to see how the pros do it. You might even start to feel better about yourself once you see how other teachers handle their classes. Administrators can offer help in other ways and may be generous with helping you get connected to people who can help you or people who share certain interests with you. It also pays to speak with administrators on a regular basis in case you need special supplies or assistance. This way they know what problems you are experiencing and that you are actively trying to resolve them and can help accordingly. School employees are generally pretty nice people, so ask for help. The worst they can do is say no, which is unlikely. As for feeling intimidated to speak up, just realize that as you gain experience, this feeling will pass. In the meantime, try getting involved with a school committee that you are interested in and learn all about it. This way you will feel that you are knowledgeable in at least one area of school life and can speak up about it. And do not forget that more experienced teachers can learn a thing or two from new teachers who are fresh from training as well!

I feel I am a victim of a major guilt trip. From all sides, I keep getting the impression that if I do not spend 24 hours a day thinking and working on school-related issues, I am not a "dedicated teacher." I believe I am doing a good job in the classroom because the kids are learning and my evaluations are great, but because I tend to limit my activities to a reasonable part of the day, I get frowned on. Am I really a bad teacher?

You have already done the first thing correctly, and that is asking yourself if your students are learning and progressing. If so, then yes, you are a good teacher. The myth that teachers are single-minded souls whose dedication to their students overrides every other consideration in their lives, such as family, friends, church, self-fulfillment, and so forth, is unfortunately still being perpetuated. There are some teachers whose life *is* their work, but the majority have a good balance. The current rallying cry is for teachers to be more professional but at the same time totally giving of all their time and resources without compensation. Have you ever seen a doctor who said, "Well, it's after office hours and I'm still working on this patient, so I guess I won't charge for my work now because of my total dedication to the profession"? Of course not! Yet we still refer to the physician as dedicated. If you can get your job done during school hours, your students are learning, the administration is happy with your work, and you are a relatively happy person, I would say you are a big success.

Chapter 2

Who, What, When, Where, and Why, Oh Why, Me?

Organization

Teachers are excellent jugglers. They manage to keep students, parents, administrators, and other teachers happy and informed while planning and delivering meaningful lessons, creating unique and stimulating assessment methods, grading the resulting papers, serving lunch and bus duty, attending parent conferences and faculty meetings, serving on numerous committees, sponsoring clubs and fund-raisers, attending professional development seminars, and taking graduate courses for recertification credit. And all of this is supposed to be accomplished with only an approximately 1-hour long planning period each day. Organization is the key to keeping all of these different balls in the air. Getting to this necessarily high level of organizational skill requires years of experience and a lot of thought. The road to the personal peace of excessive organization can be shortened somewhat by sharing ideas with other teachers. With that in mind, this chapter provides a few ideas that might help.

Planning Issues

◈◈◈

The lesson plans that I use in class are full of examples, demonstrations, facts, questions, and so forth. In short, it is too much to fit in those little blocks of the lesson plan book. Do they really expect a teacher to fit a whole class period into such a tiny square? How do I realistically do just that?

◈◈◈

I have never known what the makers of lesson plan books really had in mind when they made those tiny boxes, or, for that matter, what some administrators have in mind when they expect you to fit all of your planning into such a small space. If that is all you used, it seems to me that you would be a poor planner. Teachers who plan well keep a notebook for each subject or class filled with plans, demonstrations, questions, activities, tests, quizzes, transparencies, and so forth arranged by the day or unit. If they are teaching the same subject several years in a row, their plan book will be composed of a series of references to their subject or class notebook so that they will be able to get an overview of the flow of instruction by the week and by the month. This allows teachers to plan for several weeks in a matter of minutes. Of course, if the textbook or curriculum changes, the notebook will have to be revised. However, as long as the subject is the same, much of the lesson planning will still be usable with the new textbook or curriculum. Do not forget to add new techniques and strategies to your notebook each year as well as notations about problems you encountered with methods you used previously.

The administration wants my plans to look a certain way, but their organizational style does not meet my needs for real class planning. How can I meet my needs and theirs at the same time when both require such different things?

There is the old school joke about keeping one set of books for the administration and a *real* set for you to use. However, unless you have a really domineering administration, just explain to them how your way works better for you and that you would be happy to share with them your lesson plans done your way. If they are not agreeable, there is still no need to keep two books. Try keeping your lesson plan book according to the administration guidelines and simply come up with a coding system so that you reference your usable plans for yourself. For example, the small box in your plan book might give the unit name and number, objective, and homework. The unit name and number will act as a reference for your notebook of detailed plans that list activities, questions, examples, lecture notes, and so forth. Recording a smaller version of your true plan in your plan book can help you get a quick overview of instruction over a long period of time without the immense detail of your daily plans. In other words, your plan book becomes a date book of activities, and the real activities are referenced in the plan book but kept elsewhere.

I seem to always be a day and a page ahead of my students, my nights are full of grading papers, and my weekends are full of all the other details I must deal with. They tell me that planning is the key, but if I add detailed planning to everything else I must do, I will never sleep again! How can doing more detailed planning possibly help?

If this is your first year of teaching, what you are describing is unfortunately the trial by fire that all teachers have gone through. It gets much easier after the first year. However, if this is your 5th year of teaching or, heaven forbid, your 20th, then shame on you! You are really not taking advantage of the benefits of planning ahead. For example, if you teach the same subject out of the same book year after year, why are you not keeping a notebook with the daily lesson plans you have used and tests, quizzes, activities, and so on? Why are you reinventing the wheel every year? If you keep a notebook, you can plan for 2 weeks of work in about 5 minutes simply by referencing your teaching notebook. Schedule tests and quizzes not only for your students' benefit but also for your benefit. For example, if all of your classes happen to have tests or quizzes fall on the same day, do not kill yourself staying up all night trying to grade them all! Plan to have some of the tests as multiple choice so that you can grade them in test scoring machines in about 2 minutes while other tests can be graded during testing periods in different classes. In short, plan with yourself as well as your students in mind. When you meet with your department to discuss which courses each of you will teach the following year, make sure you request at least some of them being the same ones you have previously taught so that your planning will be done for the most part. Take advantage of your planning period as well. You can get a tremendous amount done during that time. I cannot tell you how many times I have seen teachers use this as a rest period when they chat, eat, and even take a nap! I would surely rather rest at home than at work, wouldn't you? You would be amazed at how much you can accomplish if you take advantage of every minute you are at work and relax every minute you are at home!

When I call in sick, the last thing I feel like doing is writing up lesson plans and calling them in or having them delivered. How can I call in sick and turn over and go back to sleep?

The key to a stress-free sick morning is planning ahead. You know you will be sick at some point in the year. Therefore, have a substitute folder ready in your box before the first day of school every year and label it "Sub Folder." Include the following items (which are kept up-to-date throughout the year) in your substitute folder:

- Seating charts and class rolls (Include a note to the substitute asking him or her to use these charts to document misbehavior and students who did not do assigned work.)

- Your daily schedule

- The name and room number of your department chair if problems arise

- Your home phone number in case problems arise

- Short directions about evacuation of your class in case of drills or emergencies

- A list of your weekly extra duties and the locations of those duties

- What to do about severe disciplinary problems (Include a note saying that you do not tolerate misbehavior and the substitute should not either, so he or she should feel free to remove students with disciplinary referrals, if needed.)

- Your general class rules about eating in class, bathroom passes, and so forth

- Five days of emergency plans such as the following: Work all odd-numbered problems in the next section of the book, do a standardized test practice and have the practice tests in an accessible place in your classroom, show a video related to your subject and have the students write down 20 facts they learned from it, or have students read magazines related to your subject and write synopses of two articles, including how they relate to your subject (the substitute can pick up boxes of the magazines from the library in the morning). Number these plans 1 through 5, and keep the basic idea of each plan on an index card in your wallet so that when you call for a substitute you can simply say, "Do Plan 3 today," and roll over and go back to sleep.

- A note to be read aloud to students (e.g., "All work will be checked for completeness and accuracy. Grades will be posted in the grade book for use in your averages. Failure to do the work will result in a 0. Misbehavior will be reported to me, as will students who do not do the assigned work, and appropriate action will be taken.")

Of course, you can always have someone deliver detailed plans to your school that will keep the flow of your instruction going while you are absent. But if you are really feeling like death warmed over, you probably want the comfort of knowing you can phone in a single number for a daily plan and all will be well.

Being absent from work when you are a teacher is almost not worth it! All your planning has to be redone based on what happened when you had a substitute. How can I catch up everything quickly?

There are some classes you can leave work for and rest easy because you know they will do just what you asked them to do, and there are the other 95% of classes who think substitute day is a free day. If you followed the instructions given in the previous question about leaving a thorough sub folder, your sick day should have been fairly restful and stress free. Once you come back, however, expect your first day to be one in which you review all the work you left for the kids. In your plan book, use Post-It notes that are the size of the blocks in your plan book to shift your plans forward to other days. (I have known teachers who write plans only on Post-It notes because they can easily move lessons to different days. This is not a bad idea!) Most of all, do what you said you would do when it comes to grading the work. This way, students will believe the assignments you leave for them really will count in their final grade. Finally, hand out appropriate punishments when you return and call the parents of students who misbehaved for the substitute to let the parents know that their kids were being disrespectful to a very hard-working individual.

As soon as I finish planning for the coming 2 weeks, I find out that there will be an assembly or a test for the sophomores that will have them out of class for 2 days. What is the best way to replan when this stuff happens?

❧

God's gift to teachers must be the Post-It notes. Do not be afraid to shift your plans a day ahead using moveable blocks, such as the Post-It notes mentioned in the previous question, in your plan book. If you are a high school teacher who likes to keep all similar classes on the same page each day, and you experience a disruption to only one of those classes, simply expand or contract the others as need be. For example, suppose you have three sections of Algebra I. One of those sections does not meet on its appointed day because of an assembly. Will that class be perpetually behind for the entire year? No. Simply replan the others to allow time for you to teach that missing section. The next time you meet the absentee class after the assembly you could teach the missing section just as you had originally planned while the other two classes do extra practice work on their previous day's section. In one class period, all classes will be back on track, although all your plans will have shifted forward 1 day. Above all, do not panic. Plans are not set in stone for public school teachers for precisely the reasons you mentioned. Many times we do not have control over when our classes will meet and how often. Learn to roll with the flow and come armed with your box of Post-It notes!

TIME MANAGEMENT

❧

I feel so overwhelmed with work. Surely there is a better way to manage my time. Help!

❧

The best way to deal with the overwhelming number of tasks any teacher must perform is planning, planning, and more planning. Plan for yourself as well as for the students. The question on detailed planning in the Planning section of this chapter has helpful ideas on decreasing your workload. Also, learn to say, "No, I'm too busy." There simply is not enough time in the day to do everything people want you to do. Get your priorities straight and plan accordingly. If your family comes first, plan so that you do not take home any work. (Yes, it can be done!) If your career comes first, plan so that you have ample opportunities to attend networking conferences and training seminars. Be sure that your students are always your top priority because if you are failing to meet their needs, you really need to find another line of work. Careful planning, however, will let you balance the needs of your students against the needs of yourself, your family, and your career without any noticeable sacrifices. Try to find all those extra minutes in the day that you are currently losing. If your administration requires you to stand at your door during class changes, just take a few papers to grade out in the hall with you. Lunchtime is a great time to get work done. Thirty minutes before school starts, do not sit in the lounge gossiping and drinking coffee; get some work done! Finally, have students help you when at all possible. For example, if someone finishes a test early, let him or her make copies for another class, clean off your overhead transparencies, or some other odd jobs depending on the age of your students. If you wish, reward your helpers with extra credit, candy, stickers, or something else that is age-appropriate. All of these techniques combined will help you feel a little less overwhelmed.

I am constantly being asked to be on different committees, substitute for absent teachers during my planning period, sponsor clubs, coordinate events, and the list goes on and on. When am I supposed to do all this stuff and teach as well?

Unlike other jobs where employees have break times and hour-long lunches, teachers work from the moment they open the school door until they leave. (And if you have been taking the advice of this book, you will not work much at home!) Every second is occupied during the day. As has been stated before, planning is the key to managing your workload and pleasing all your clients, whether they are students, administrators, or parents. All the responsibilities you mentioned in the question are natural, albeit time-consuming, parts of a teaching position, so you might as well look on the bright side. Every teacher usually should sponsor a club if for no other reason than they get to do something they are interested in and present a different side of themselves to students. They also get to know their students in a different way. Choose your committees, if you can, to advance yourself professionally and to show off your knowledge in specific areas. Coordinating events is a great way to demonstrate your organizational and managerial skills if you are hoping to move into administration. Substituting for other teachers is not very advantageous to you and is usually more of a nuisance than anything else. However, due to the nationwide shortage of substitutes, it is becoming more and more a necessary evil. If you and your colleagues who substitute frequently during planning organize yourselves and present a unified front, perhaps your administration will find an alternative or maybe you will be paid additional money. It never hurts to ask!

Class Routines

𐕕𐕖

What is the best way to keep a grade book so that I can easily access student grades and averages quickly?

𐕕𐕖

If you have an established grade policy where you weight different types of grades, you probably need to group those grades in your grade book. For example, you may have columns 1 through 20 devoted to quizzes, columns 25 through 30 for tests, and columns 35 through 45 for daily work. Even if you do not weight grades, be sure to arrange the grade book in a manner that is easiest for you to average quickly, and be sure you list the date of the assignment at the top of each column as well as the assignment itself. This way you can answer student and parent questions about scores or missing assignments more quickly. As far as posting periodic averages, you might wish to keep the interim average in your grade book because it is a good indicator of how students are doing at the halfway mark. Also, keep each student's marking period averages at the end of the row for that student. This way at the end of the year you can do final averages quickly. This will also help you to tell parents how their child is progressing throughout the year. A computerized grade book program that suits your needs for averaging will really be worth the extra time it takes to record grades in two places. The only drawback of a computerized grading program is that some teachers feel less connected to their students' grades when the computer does the averaging than when the teacher manually goes through the process. Some teachers dislike losing the review of a student's performance they experience when averaging grades manually. Regardless of whether you have such a program, you still need a portable record of student grades to take with you to conferences and meetings.

೧೭

How does one establish a grading policy?

೧೭

Usually a district has a general grading policy regarding assignment of letter grades, whether behavior can count for or against grade assignments, how many grades you should have prior to the end of a marking period, and so forth. The districts usually leave the particulars of grading up to the individual departments or teachers. If you have some control over your grading policy, it makes sense to categorize the assignments you might give during the year and weight them differently. For example, quizzes may count once with the lowest grade dropped each marking period, tests may count twice and cannot be dropped, projects or reports may count three times, and the homework average may count as a major test. The point system also works well as long as you do not try to predict the total number of points possible in a 9-week period. It is hard for secondary and elementary teachers to predict exactly how many quizzes or tests they may give in a marking period because public schools are prone to interruptions during the school year, such as unannounced assemblies or field trips, that may cause half of your class to be absent. Also, conscientious teachers have a tendency to reteach and retest material when the scores warrant, thus making it difficult to predict the number of assessments in a marking period. If you are using a point system, simply let your students know how much each individual task is worth rather than the total number of points for the entire grading period.

❋

What is the best way to keep track of attendance and to notify parents if their child is having a problem in that area?

❋

Check with your school first. They may have a system, computerized or otherwise, that already handles this for you. If not, be sure you include an up-to-date attendance record on all grade reports sent home to parents. In addition, it is a good idea to have a stack of forms you have prepared in advance specifically for the purpose of notifying parents of attendance problems if your school does not handle this in some other way. These forms should have spaces for student name, class, teacher name, and the number of tardies and absences for each student. Be sure you have a notation on the form that states the legal number of absences for semester and yearlong classes in your state. Mail one of these completed forms to the parent at periodic intervals, such as the student's 3rd, 5th, and 10th absence, and be sure you keep a copy for yourself. This way you have proof of notification if parents claim that you did not keep them informed of their children's absences. (Resist the urge to tell parents that it is *their* job to keep track of whether their children attend school regularly!) Even if your school handles all the attendance issues for you, make sure you keep your own personal attendance record for verification purposes.

❋

My students want to sit where they please. Is this OK?

❋

You need a seating chart for a variety of reasons. It is much quicker to take attendance when you can simply spot which desks are empty and note those students who are absent. When you have a substitute, a seating chart is an invaluable tool for them in maintaining discipline and identifying troublemakers. Finally, the most important reason to have a seating chart is to control the class's behavior, and you can do that only by regulating the interaction of students through their proximity to each other. However, when creating seating charts, be sure that you change them periodically throughout the year because students who were not friends before you sat them next to each other can become extremely close, talkative friends after awhile. Also be sure to consider students with poor eyesight or hearing as well as students who might actually behave violently when seated next to certain other students.

We begin every class by going over the previous night's homework, but I have 150 students and not always much time to check to make sure they actually did it. What are some quick ways to assign a grade for completion of homework?

Surprise inspections are best because students know they must do their homework every day for fear of getting caught without it. One of the best ways to check for homework is to take a few minutes of class time and have students leave their work out on their desk so you can spot check it. However, the disadvantage of this method is that there are many ways students can fool the teacher. For example, if you assigned seven questions to be answered for homework, be sure you check questions number 2 and 7 to see if the work that is on their desk is actually the work for that day. Also be alert to students passing around the same homework page so that when you get to their desk you have already seen the same assignment five times. Put some sort of mark on the homework itself as a note to yourself that you have already seen it. As far as grading homework during a spot check, you might assign a check for completing the assignment, a half-check for completing approximately half, and a 0 for failure to complete. Another way to check homework quickly is a home-work quiz. This is also done without a prior announcement and can be taken up and graded as a regular quiz. For example, your quiz might be the following: "On January 22, in the homework for Section 5-2, what was the answer to question 12?" This has many advantages because the students must date their work, keep it in order, and be sure they have copied the correct answers to problems or questions if they got it wrong on their homework when you went over it in class. It is also very quick to grade, and in fact, you can have students exchange papers and grade it for you, which saves even more time.

How do I establish a classroom routine that meets my needs and those of my students?

You need to think ahead about possible classroom scenarios and have routines worked out either in your mind or on paper. For example, how will you handle requests for bathroom privileges and the many urgent requests for going to the nurse, library, phone, other teachers, main office, coaches, guidance, and so forth? How will you quickly take attendance, record tardies, check homework, ensure against cheating during tests, have stu-dents work together in groups during class, and so forth? As you gain more experience at teaching, much of this will become second nature. However, as a beginning teacher, you really need to take time during the course of several days and think of possible situations that could arise so that you are not taken aback with indecision when they occur. Also, develop basic routines for different types of lessons. For example, the following is a suggestion for a day on which you plan to lecture: Take attendance, introduce the topic for the day on the overhead or chalkboard, go over homework, teach the lesson with examples and demonstrations, assign group work to students and check the group work, have students come to the front to explain, review the lesson, and assign homework. Different routines will be needed for days on which you do group work, projects, tests, and so forth. If you plan to do something out of the ordinary on a particular day, be sure you think through the routine of how you are going to manage it along with the possible pitfalls and problems and how you will handle them.

CORRESPONDENCE

&

I have 150 students and each parent wants to be informed the minute their child fails a quiz or test. What is the most expedient way to keep everyone notified and happy?

&

In elementary school, you need to put the responsibility for communication on the parent. Let parents know at the beginning of the year what day or days you will be sending a collection of their child's work home in a folder. Leave a blank page in the folder for parents to sign that they have seen the work and to write comments and concerns to you. In middle and high schools, you are going to have to put the burden on the student.

Invest in a red ink pad and a stamp that says "Parental Signature Required." If students fail a quiz or test, send home the assignment with the red stamp on the top. If they fail to bring it back, tell them that their grade drops by 10 points for each day they fail to bring it back, and after a couple of days, call the parents if the test is not returned. If lowering students' grades will not work in your district because of restrictions on removal of points from students because of behavior, you will need to devise some other methods of ensuring that the tests are signed. Another suggestion would be to have the signature count as a homework assignment and then give students a 0 on it if they fail to return the test within 2 days. Be sure you keep the original tests or copies of the tests where parental signatures were required in case the issue of forgery comes up. (Helpful hint: To make keeping tests and quizzes less of a hassle for you, have students put their names on manila folders on the first day of class and collect them alphabetically so that all you have to do is pop the offending tests into their file when the need arises. Less work on your part!) Another way to keep parents informed is to have a form students must maintain in their notebooks that keeps track of their grades for each 9-week period. You can do spot checks, similar to homework checks, to make sure that they are keeping their grade lists current. Inform parents at the beginning of the year that such a grade list is available constantly should they be interested in a record of their child's performance. Regardless of what grade you teach, make sure that parents know how to contact you by phone, postal mail, email, or voice mail and that you are happy to respond to any concerns or comments they may have.

Is it really necessary to keep up with all my parent contacts? If it is, what is the easiest way to do it?

Yes, it is really necessary that you keep up with your parent contacts. You may need to prove the case to your principal or even your district office that you have actually attempted to contact parents and inform them of what is happening in your class. If you have records of contacts, you can prove your case and end these discussions very quickly. This happened to me once when a parent claimed to have never been notified, and I produced a paper trail of contacts as long as my arm. Although the parent had come to school with the intention of blasting my inadequacies as a teacher, the meeting was over in 5 minutes. It is a simple matter to keep track of this sort of thing: Just follow the suggestions in the previous question about keeping a folder on each student and drop a little piece of paper in that student's file every time you attempt to or succeed in contacting a parent. You might also keep a journal of your parent contacts. Regardless of how you decide to do it, keep track of all attempts to contact, whether you left messages, and the final outcome. Again, you never know when you will need the proof.

Is there a need to keep track of all the small pieces of paper that deal with a student throughout a year? I am referring to passes out of class, late notes from other teachers, innocuous guidance notifications, and that sort of thing.

Oddly enough, the answer is yes! If it is at all possible, have a small file cabinet by your desk with a manila folder for each student, as has been mentioned previously. Drop into each folder any piece of paper you receive that deals with that student, whether it is tests returned with parental signatures, grade reports, or passes into and out of class. For example, you never know when a student will be involved in something where you will have to prove that a particular student was or was not in your class when some incident occurred. You may need proof that a student has stolen guidance conference forms and has been forging them to get out of class. You may need to prove to a parent that you sent home tests to be signed when they claim they never saw them, and you may uncover a student forger. If you never need these pieces of paper, throw them out at the end of the year. Chances are you will never need them, but the one time you do need them they will really be invaluable.

3

A Little Song, A Little Dance, A Little Quiz Tomorrow

Delivery of Lessons and Student Assessments

Think back for a moment to your own life as a student. As a student, how many times did you experience total confusion and bewilderment in classes with one teacher, whereas in a different class with another teacher, you learned similar subject matter easily and confidently? That is the difference between teaching subject matter and teaching students. A good teacher knows the elements that go into the delivery of lessons that involve and inform students in such a way as to promote maximum understanding and retention. Furthermore, an excellent educator understands that the assessment of students is an integral part of the lesson itself and designs these evaluations accordingly. Fortunately, there is no great mystery surrounding these twin pillars of teaching. Although the grand scope of teaching methods and ideas form a brilliant tapestry, the fundamentals of good teaching run through it like a bright wide ribbon: Although much color, texture, and style can be added to the basics, there is no denying their underlying supporting structure in any teacher's delivery of lessons and assessment of students.

The Act of Teaching

Is there any formula for being sure that lessons are delivered well? I am a science teacher so I like to follow formulas, but I have heard the saying, "You know good teaching when you see it" so many times I could scream!

Good lesson delivery involves the following basic elements, regardless of the subject or the teacher:

1. A brief review of the previous day's work.

2. Some sort of opening illustration or demonstration that captures the attention of the class and pertains to the current day's topic.

3. The presentation of the objective for the day, perhaps phrased in the form of a question that the students should be able to answer at the end of the day's lesson if they have truly learned it.

4. A reason for why the topic is important to learn or how it is used in everyday life.

5. The content for the day presented in a variety of strategies designed to appeal to different styles of learning. For

example, you may briefly go over the homework from the night before and tie it to today's lesson, answer questions, present the topic of the day in a short lecture format, have the students participate in some sort of guided learning activity (of which the varieties are endless), and then have a group discussion about the topic and what was learned from the activity.

6. Review the day's lesson by rereading the objective or the basic question of the day (or better yet, have the students read it aloud). Have students comment on the importance of the topic, ask leading review questions of the students, and stress the particular points that were made that were especially important.

7. Evaluate the students in some way, such as by giving surprise or announced quizzes or tests, asking probing questions, having them write down the answer to the basic question of the day, having them explain to each other key concepts, or simply through providing some sort of assignment that they can practice at home and see how well they do for themselves.

(Helpful hint: If you follow this pattern, write out your lesson plans to follow it and decide how much time you are going to allot to each part based on the length of time of your class periods. As you grow in experience, you will find that you can deviate from this pattern and still be effective. Nevertheless, it is an excellent platform from which to launch your lessons.)

I hear myself teaching, and I see students taking notes. However, their ability to recall information on tests is about zero, and their actual understanding seems nonexistent.

How can I get them to remember and understand so that
they will not only perform well on tests but also actually
know something when they are done?

࿇

Frequent reviews during a single class period, weekly and
monthly reviews, and lots of student participation are the
answers. The key is that you *guide* the reviews, you do not *do*
them yourself. For example, you can stop every 10 minutes or so
in a class period and have the student on the right turn to the
student on the left and explain a concept to him or her. The student on the left gets to make the judgment about whether the
other student was correct, and then the same students switch for
another concept. You can have students write the answers to the
basic questions for the class period and read them aloud so that
the class can discuss their correctness and completeness. You
also can assign group work on practice problems where the
groups are structured in such a way as to have a range of student
abilities in them: one high-skilled student, one low-skilled
student, and two average-skilled students. This way, students
can speak freely and have at least one in the group who is pretty
sure of being able to explain things. Another option is to assign
different sections to different students to teach as a review for
the class periodically throughout the year, and this can count as
a project grade. This works really well if you have a rubric ready
(see the second part of this chapter) so that students know what
they are being graded on, and it also provides structure for the
students in their first expedition into teaching. Over the years,
many students have told me that they never really learned material until they had to teach it themselves, so I am convinced of
the retention and understanding benefits of this method. Finally,
do not forget that hands-on experiences produce far more retention than lecture experiences.

These are just a few examples. Entire books could be written
on the countless ways a teacher can provide retention and

reinforcement activities for students. If you think about it, you are sure to come up with some methods that will suit you and your students.

∞◆∞

I am stuck in a lecture rut. Can you give me some ideas of ways to liven up my classes? Even I am bored hearing myself talk!

∞◆∞

If you are bored, think about your poor students! You may be the 6th hour of lectures they have heard in a single day! Lectures have their place; after all, you have to actually spend some time dispensing knowledge. However, there are many reinforcing activities that can be utilized. You might want to check out the question in this section on retention activities to find some ways to spice up your lecture. In addition, try giving the students projects to do that are meaningful and require them to tie together large blocks of knowledge. Hopefully, these projects will require students to work together cooperatively, present a final result (papers, constructions, equations, etc.), and get out of their chairs! Have students take on part of the job of instruction. Let them devise clever and interesting ways to explain concepts or problems, even on a daily basis. Also, let them write the tests themselves by submitting questions to you, and if their questions are accepted, they can receive bonus points on that test. If you show movies or videos, be sure to have students write down 10 or more facts that they learned from them and provide an analysis of the concepts presented in the film as well as a personal critique of the production itself. Check out the practice of cooperative learning. It works extremely well, and if done in its complete glory (team names and logos, tournaments, etc.), it can be a real morale booster in class. Technology can also provide a great break from lecturing in addition to motivating students to learn. Whatever alternative paths you decide to take, promise yourself that you will limit yourself to 10 or 15 minutes per day of lecture, and think of ways that you can involve students personally in activities. After all, if you provide 10 or 15 minutes of wall-to-wall new knowledge, you need to provide 45 minutes to an hour of practice and reinforcement time to let the students understand and retain the information. It is really worth the effort to expand their involvement time and lessen your lecture time because the increased learning will be phenomenal.

Student Assessments

What are rubrics exactly and how do I communicate them to students and write them for myself so that they do not look like small versions of the U.S. tax code?

The simplest way to think about rubrics is to think about how students use them. Rubrics are simply outlines of how you intend to grade their product, whatever that may be. If you are looking for certain things to be present in order to assign an A, tell them so. Let students know ahead of time how much you intend to count off for various missing aspects. In essence, the rubric is a guide for how you want the content of their product to be presented to receive an A, including the quality of the content. If you write a rubric like some of the staff development guest speakers want you to do, you will spend more time writing it than you will grading your students' papers. The simpler the rubric, the more the students will be able to follow what they are supposed to do. So my bottom-line advice is to make the rubric student friendly, and do not make it so that you have boxed yourself in a corner as far as the grading goes.

❦

I think open-ended questions and short-term projects are ideal ways to learn. However, they take me forever to grade! How can I make it so that I get a quicker turn-around on this type of assignment?

❦

There are two ways that I have used that make it a quick grade, even though the project may be long. For some projects, you may wish to provide students with an outline where they fill in the different parts of their answers so you do not have to go hunting for the different sections in a long and rambling narrative form. For other projects, you may wish to make out a sheet for yourself in which you have a list of the items you are looking for and numbers out to the side of each detailing the degree to which the student presented that answer (e.g., 3 means 3 points for stating it correctly, 2 means 2 points for getting it correct but there are grammar or spelling errors, 1 point means the answer itself is only partially correct, and 0, of course, means it is wrong.) This way you are grading each child fairly and according to the same scale. It is not a bad idea to give each student a copy of this paper in advance and have them attach it to the front of their project. This way they know what is expected of them and you have the small, but not insignificant, bonus of not having to attach it to their papers yourself!

❦

I like to use essays on my math tests so that I can have students explain concepts or procedures. I feel this tells me more than just their solutions. However, students and even their parents rebel against this because they say that this has no place in a math class. I should mention I take points for spelling, grammar, and punctuation errors as well. What is your opinion?

Essays are great on math tests because they really require students to engage in metacognition—that is, thinking about how they think about math problems. Do not back down on this practice because it really shows how much students understand math and not just that they can go through the motions of working routine problems. Furthermore, counting off for spelling is totally legitimate. If a child cannot spell *Pythagorean Theorem*, that should be considered part of his or her math knowledge and graded accordingly. Grammar and punctuation are a different story. If you take the view that English is a separate subject and should not be graded in a math class, then you will not count off. If, however, you take a more global approach to education and feel that each discipline should support the other, you will confer with the English teacher and count off for grammar and punctuation. It is dependent on which view you hold, but you should let the students know in advance so that they are not taken aback when they get their results and so that you will not have a lot of explaining to do after the fact.

I think pop quizzes keep students on their toes. However, most of my colleagues tend to favor announced quizzes. Is there some rule on this or is it every teacher for himself or herself?

It is every teacher for himself or herself. Some people now believe that if you want students to learn certain things, you spell out what it is you want them to be able to do on tests so that they know where to focus their energies. Their rationale is, "Why hide what it is you want students to be able to accomplish? Let them know up front what you expect them to do." The flip side, of course, is the school of thought that says students should learn and understand everything the teacher imparts to them and should study accordingly so that they are ready for any eventuality. This shows that they have truly mastered the entire content of the course instead of just being taught possible questions on their tests. Personally, I can see both sides of the issue. If you are a fence-straddler like me, you could let your students know in advance to expect unannounced pop quizzes. Use your judgment regarding the makeup of your classes. Perhaps some of them would benefit from the first approach, which is more structured, whereas more advanced classes would benefit from the second approach, which is more like college classes. It is really a judgment call.

Students are always asking for extra credit. I feel that they should worry about the credit first before they ask for "extra credit." Is it OK not to accept extra credit from students?

Whether to give extra credit is definitely your prerogative. It is OK to let them know up front that the points they will be receiving will be only from quizzes, test, projects, and so forth. However, you might want to rethink your position. You can sometimes coax extra work out of students with the promise of extra points. Read on to the next question for some good ideas about extra credit. It might change your mind.

I like to give extra credit. However, I do not particularly like reports copied out of the encyclopedia on famous scientists. What are some ideas of interesting and fun ways to give extra credit and have the students advance their learning at the same time?

Extra credit can be used as payment for students. You can "pay" them points for working homework problems on the board or for explaining concepts to other students. You also can have students work out problems for the class when they get tests back instead of your having to do it. You can offer "extra credit days" when you assign work you probably would have done anyway, such as puzzles dealing with scientific formulas, and offer a certain amount of points per sheet or per problem. You can assign classwork to groups, let students turn in one paper for the group, and then give each member of the group a certain amount of points per correct answer. One of my favorite ways to offer extra credit is the "review game." The following outlines how you play it:

- Have students count off 1 through 6 (or however many sections you are testing on).

- Based on the number they were assigned, each student writes 3 to 5 questions for that section, making sure that a certain number of them are conceptual (e.g., analysis, explanations) and a certain number of them are simple problems (e.g., numerical answers, definitions).

- Place these questions into a stack. There should also be stack of index cards with student names on them.

- Draw a set of students' questions out of the stack. A student comes up to the front and draws a name out of the index cards. He or she asks that student one of the questions. If the student can answer within 1 minute, he or she gets 3 points. If not, then the student asking the questions can choose another student who has his or her hand up. If that student can answer, he or she gets 3 points. If not, then the student asking the questions has to answer the question, and then he or she gets the 3 points. After that student has finished asking all of the questions, he or she draws another set of student questions out of the stack, another student comes up, and so the play continues.

Students get really excited about this game; it is a great way to review for quizzes with minimal work on your part, and it is a legitimate way to award extra credit points.

Take a Deep Breath and Count to 10 Before Yelling

Discipline and Classroom Management

If you ask teachers what they love about teaching, you will get a variety of delightful answers. If you ask teachers what they dislike about teaching, you will probably get one overwhelming answer: discipline. It seems that every year, students arrive in class with less understanding of proper classroom behavior and even less interest in learning it. Many times, a teacher must not only instruct their students in the content, but must also teach them manners and respect. Unfortunately, you have to get their attention before you can do that, and in some classes, this is a task in and of itself. In the area of discipline and classroom management, experience is the best source of information, so in this chapter you will find some real situations and solutions that helped manage those classes.

Whole-Class Discipline Issues

∞

What can I do to establish good discipline in my classroom?

∞

The first minute of the first day of school, immediately establish your expectations for the class. This includes academic expectations as well as your classroom rules, punishments for disobeying the rules, and hopefully, rewards for good behavior as well. It is very important, however, that you really mean what you say. If you say that you will require 15 minutes of lunch detention if a student is not in his or her seat when the bell rings, do it and do it consistently. Consistency, particularly at the beginning of the year, is vital to establishing discipline. If you are inconsistent, you will be perceived as not truly caring whether students behave. Inconsistency will also lead to accusations of being unfair because you punish one student on Monday but do not punish another student for the same infraction on Wednesday. Being consistent shows that you mean business about maintaining order in the classroom.

∞

I am having a lot of trouble focusing on the lesson I am trying to teach and simultaneously dealing with discipline in the classroom. If I focus on teaching, then the class gets so unruly that it is pointless to be teaching at all. If I focus on discipline, then I never get through my lesson. Help!

∞

First of all, relax. You are not alone. This is a universal problem
that affects 100% of teachers at some point in their careers.
Experience will enable you to get very good at mentally running on two tracks at the same time. When you become more
comfortable with your lessons and teaching in general, the time
you spend focusing on those aspects and the time you focus on
what is happening in the class will be more balanced. However,
you must live through the first few years to gain that experience. Take the burden of managing the entire lesson off yourself
for a while so that you can practice using the discipline techniques in this section that are appropriate for your class. How
do you put the responsibility for the lesson elsewhere when you
are the teacher? Involve your students actively in the class by
having them explain problems, do group work, and even teach
ideas to their classmates. You will find other ways to involve
students more in your classes in Chapter 3's question about getting out of the lecture rut. However you do it, you periodically
put the burden of the lesson primarily on the students so that
you can focus on the discipline problems and, hopefully, nip
them in the bud!

In school, we were taught assertive discipline techniques
that involved tracking the progressively bad behavior of
individual disruptive students in a class. This works fine for
me in classes in which only 1 or 2 kids are causing a problem, but what can a teacher do when it is 25 out of 30
kids who are causing the problem?

Recognize that no student can learn in this type of environment,
and the teacher will not be able to maintain their sanity or dignity for long either. It is very possible that none of these kids

want to learn what you are teaching, but maybe there is one who does. Would you really want your own child trying to learn in this type of situation every day? Of course not, it is not fair. Focus on that one child who wants to learn, and let that child be your inspiration to target all the others for discipline. After a class, reflect for a minute and then decide which five students were absolutely the worst, the instigators, so to speak. Target only them for discipline the next day. Watch their every move and take severe and swift measures such as removing them from your class for that day with punishment. Call their parents and make life hard for them in whatever means you have available. Remember, the key words are *top five students* and *swift discipline*. Continue this process every day by adding one more student to your target list of kids and discipline them each day as well. When they complain that they were doing only what the rest of the class was doing and that you are being unfair, simply point out that this line of reasoning does not work with policemen, so it will not work with you either. You may not catch all the fish in the sea in a day, but you will catch your five! This is a case of winning by attrition: divide and conquer. There is a chance you will run into some hard-case students such as the one mentioned in the next section. In this case, you may need to try different tactics, but the majority of students will see you mean business and respond accordingly. If not, enlist the help of parent volunteers, administrators, other teachers, and so forth. It worked great for me to have a parent take an hour off work to sit with their severely disruptive child during class. He was never a problem again. You might also take students to a phone after class and let them tell their parents what they just did in your class. Other extreme measures include placing running tape recorders at strategic locations in the classroom with the "off" button inoperative, videotaping the classroom, or taking pictures of the class to send home to parents. I know this is a rough situation that is all too common now, and my thoughts are with you and I hope this helps.

I was evaluated recently and received low marks for the
noise level in my classroom. I was told that I needed to
discipline the students more in this area. But the noise
level does not bother me; it is a low murmur at times, and
I feel a lot of it is caused by the students discussing what
is going on in class. Why do I have to discipline for something that I do not feel needs changing?

Every teacher has some things that do not bother them that would
drive someone else up the wall. However, this is one time you
might want to rethink your attitude toward the situation. From
where you are standing, the noise may be a low murmur, but from
the standpoint of the students who are sitting directly in front of
or beside the people doing the "low talking," it can be a major dis-
traction. It is really unfair for some students to be able to give their
undivided attention to the teacher while others are being bom-
barded with the conversations of classmates. Your job as a teacher
is not only to provide good instruction and learning experiences
but also to make the environment itself conducive to learning. The
person who evaluated you probably was sitting in the midst of the
low talkers and found that it distracted from the lesson. So in this
instance I believe this is a problem you should address with your
class. Let them know that there are times to help others with problems and times to talk, such as with group work or activities, but
lecture periods are the times to be quiet. Make this your rule and
enforce it regularly. I believe your students will appreciate it.
Besides, low murmurs may quickly become loud noises. Read on!

I understand the need to get the class's attention before
I begin instruction, but I cannot do even this because the
noise level is so loud. I have to shout over them to get

their attention, and my shouting just escalates throughout the period. I go home every day with a sore throat. What can I do to get them quiet at the start of class and save my vocal cords?

Unfortunately, this is a pretty common problem these days. You must let students know you mean business. But how to do this if they ignore the fact that you are there in the first place? First of all, *never shout.* Talk quietly and they will often hush each other so that they can hear you. For a hard-case class, call the parents of the worst offenders, and let them know about their child's disrespect. Be sure that the students know you are more than willing to call back to report their progress, whether good or bad. Word of this will spread throughout the class and it should be quieter. Put a sign on your board that states the following: "If you are not in your seat, quiet, and ready to begin when the bell rings, you will receive a disciplinary referral and be temporarily removed from this class." Then follow through and have a stack of referrals ready. If you have an assistant principal for discipline or discipline monitors, have them sit in your class to get the students quiet initially, or have the monitors speak to your class about the disciplinary consequences of their extreme loudness. Do not try to teach until you have this problem under control, even if it means writing up each student and ejecting him or her from class until there are only two students left. You have a serious problem, so do not let it continue because you will not get any teaching done, and you will come to hate your job because of this problem. Try these techniques, and if none of them work, ask administrators and other teachers to help. It never hurts to get a few more ideas.

My classes are generally pretty good discipline wise. However, in a few classes there are one or two "bad eggs." They ruin the atmosphere for the whole class with their wisecracks and negative comments as well as, at times, outright misbehavior. What can I do to get them to straighten up?

When dealing with students like these, never confront them in front of the class. You will be considered the enemy and their classmates will usually side with them. Talk to them before or after class in a quiet place where it is just the two of you. Explain the problems that their behavior is causing and how you will not tolerate it. Ask them if there is a problem that causes their misbehavior that you can help solve. Try to get them to see your side of things; in other words, do not yell but coerce. The old saying that you catch more flies with honey than vinegar really works. If, however, the kids are truly the hard-line troublemakers who are consistently disruptive, you have several options. First, target them for disciplinary action every day. Document their behavior daily and take immediate and severe disciplinary action according to your school policy. Either they will eventually wear down or you will have enough ammunition to have them removed from your class, and possibly the school itself, if the problems are severe and frequent enough. Talk to other teachers about the troublemakers and find out if they are misbehaving in those classes as well. If so, ask the other teachers to take the same hard line, which will add to the legal fuel required to remove the student from your class or the school.

When a student does something that I consider misbehaving in some way, should I correct him or her in front of their classmates or step outside with the student and risk having something happen in the classroom while I am out?

As a general rule, never confront a student in the presence of his or her peers. He or she will be defensive, and he or she will generally be supported by classmates. However, you do not need to leave the room because just walking quietly to his or her desk and speaking in a low tone may be enough. If you think your class has sufficient maturity, take the student outside and speak with him or her, but you will want to position your body in the doorway so that one ear is with your class and the other ear is with the misbehaving student. You always have another option if the student is being extremely obnoxious. You can simply have him or her go to whatever containment area your school has for severely misbehaving students.

Discipline in classrooms is so bad nowadays that infractions such as sleeping, note passing, not having materials, and so forth are not even a disciplinary issue anymore. When I have referred students for these behaviors, I was basically laughed at and told that disciplinary referrals were more for problems such as fighting, drugs, and sexual harassment issues. How do I discipline students for infractions that are no longer considered important?

I have only one rule in my classroom and it is this: *Students must refrain from any action or behavior that inhibits my teaching or other students' learning.* This basically sums up everything that could possibly bother me as a teacher. If sleeping, note passing, and the like bother you and keep you from doing your job or prevent other students from learning, then it is important! It sounds like your administration needs a wake-up call to support its teachers and enforce a standard of acceptable conduct for all students. If you can get them to realize this and support you, you will have no problem. If not, then you need to let students know that these behaviors will not be tolerated in your classroom, and you should also let them know what *you* will do about it if the behaviors occur. For example, you could deduct extra credit points, assign lunch or recess detention in your room, phone parents, assign additional work, and so forth. Keep records and let students know that should the misbehavior continue, you will recommend that they receive a formal disciplinary referral and its consequences, which may be in-school or out-of-school suspension. Insist that your administration treat these habitual misbehaviors as seriously as they would one episode of fighting. Follow up on the referrals you send to the administration and insist that action be taken. If you encounter nothing but resistance and apathy from your administration, perhaps it is time to think about finding another school where your viewpoints on student discipline are more commonly shared.

My classroom is very long and narrow and it is hard to see what is going on in the back from where I am standing. There always seems to be something happening, but by the time I get back there, whatever it was seems to have stopped except for some giggles and grins from the students. What can I do to stop this?

It sounds like you have some disrespectful students who need to be disciplined swiftly and consistently and seated at the front of the room under your watchful gaze. Move them immediately and discipline them every time they speak without permission or otherwise misbehave. They will quickly get the idea that you are not playing when it comes to maintaining order in your class. To allow them to remain where they are and constantly pull the wool over your eyes is to lose control of your class and abandon your authority. Surely you must know at least one of the kids who is causing the problems, so make plans to target him or her that day and either discipline or seat the student alone for the day if he or she does anything out of line. Finally, who says you have to arrange your room in a long and narrow fashion? Turn your desks so that you have more rows but they are shorter, or angle the desks so that you can see everyone. In short, design your room for maximum supervision and the student's maximum line of sight.

I feel fairly sure that some students in my class cheat on tests, but I have never been able to catch them at it. Other students have complained that these students are cheating off of them and have requested to be moved, so I did that. A lot of times their answers are the same as their neighbor's, but not for every problem on every test. What should I do?

There are many tactics to handle this. One tactic is direct confrontation if you suspect collusion between two students. After class, call them to your desk, compare papers, and get them to explain how the answers were so incredibly similar. Many times, one or both will admit cheating, and you can follow through with your school's policy. If they do not admit it, forewarn them that you suspect them of cheating, that you will be looking particularly at them, and that they are giving the perceptions of cheating to everyone. Another tactic is simply to watch them closely during the test for signs of wandering eyes; dropped paper; cheat sheets; information written on hands, sleeves, or soles of shoes; formulas typed into or taped onto calculators; and so on and nail them on the spot. A final tactic would be to reseat the entire class with special attention given to the suspected cheaters. Either seat them so that they will be at the front (directly beneath your gaze during tests), or seat them surrounded by people who usually do poorly. This way they know that they do not really have anyone to cheat off of!

Cases of Individual Student Discipline Problems

I have one student who has been subjected to every punishment available at my school, his parents have been called in for numerous conferences, and I have moved him from every seat in the classroom in an effort to improve his behavior. After I had him removed from my room for disruptive behavior, he informed me on his way out that there was nothing I could do to make him change his behavior. What do you do with a kid like that?

There are some kids who have seen and done it all, and your meager attempts at punishment have absolutely no effect. These are the hard-core cases, and I truly believe you are going to need your best personal judgment on how to handle them. You might try having a one-to-one conversation (no peers present) with this student about why he or she is behaving this way, how it affects your ability to teach, the problems that his or her behavior is causing for you, how you could be of more help to him or her, and so on. In short, talk to the student like he or she was a real person in need of some help, which he or she is. I tried this with a student in similar circumstances, and it made all the difference in the world that someone treated him with some respect instead of just piling on more punishment. Sometimes praising whatever good qualities the student possesses will also help bring him or her more in line. However, there are some kids in the world who are just incorrigible and recalcitrant and will resist every attempt at controlling their behavior. These are the kids that you try to have removed from your class and placed elsewhere. If they are aged 18 years or older, they could be placed into adult education. Repeated disciplinary referrals for younger students could cause them to be placed in special disciplinary schools or even result in expulsion from school altogether. It is a hard fact for many teachers to accept, but some students cannot be reached— no matter how hard and earnestly you try—because they do not want to be reached. If you can take the time to help this type of student change his or her ways, then great, but do not forget that you have numerous other students who need you and want your help as well.

I have a student in one class who makes me nervous from the time the class begins because I never know if this is going to be the day this kid will blow up. I feel I am a servant to this child because I am scared to do anything that will set her off. I also make sure I answer all her questions first and almost to the exclusion of other students just so that she is comfortable with everything and calm before proceeding. I lavishly praise her repeatedly for every little thing each day just for fear of having her explode! I will breathe a sigh of relief when she graduates. Her blowups are legendary and can cause the whole class to be in an uproar because she incites them to join her. What can I do to keep her under control and at the same time maintain some level of dignity for myself?

It seems as though we always have at least one student we have to tiptoe around: the student mentioned in the question above, the student with the sue-happy lawyer parent who likes to constantly threaten, or the child who makes up petitions to have teachers fired because he does not like the way they teach. If you are able to keep this student under control, then keep up the good job. In the meantime, talk to this student's other teachers and see if she behaves this way in all of her classes. If so, have her evaluated by the school psychologist to determine if she can be moved into a special program that would help her. Above all, do not be scared! So what if she blows up? Let her do it. Write down everything she says and does, keep a file for documentation purposes, and ask the other teachers she encounters daily to do the same. Chances are that if she is sufficiently unstable and causes enough frequent disruptions, she can be referred to some sort of special school or program in your district. The transfer would depend on whether she is really in need of some special attention because of an emotional problem or is just a persistent troublemaker. Just remember that your dignity is not dependent on the tantrums of a teenage girl or boy. Do what you have to do every day to teach your class in a professional manner and do not let this student get to you.

I have one student who is very bright and extremely likable and personable when I talk with him one-on-one. Yet this same nice kid turns into a complete jerk in class and mocks me and my actions while at the same time asking and answering very intelligent questions. What is going on and how can I get him to behave like a nice kid all the time?

Because your student is a nice person (as you say), then in one of your one-on-one discussions with him you should bring up this subject and ask him to behave himself. Talk to him about why he acts this way: Is he trying to be accepted by his peers? Is he trying to handle being so bright? Let him know the effect his behavior has on your opinion of him, on the class as a whole, and on any possible future repercussions such as filling out college recommendations for him. If this does not work (and sometimes it doesn't), then you simply have to treat the student as he is presenting himself: a dual personality. Discipline him effectively, fairly, and consistently in class and treat him like a nice guy in one-on-one situations. After all, he is forcing people to react to him in two ways; you are just following his lead!!

Discipline From the Teacher's Viewpoint

I am known as a strict disciplinarian. I lay down the law, and anyone who steps out of line at all is punished. However, I am increasingly finding myself confronted with argumentative and belligerent students and now even their parents are joining in the act. Whatever happened to respect for a teacher's authority to discipline in his or her classroom?

There is nothing wrong with being a strict disciplinarian. However, I have two questions for you. One question is whether you are sweating the small stuff. For example, if one student asks another for a pencil during your lecture, is that grounds for after-school detention? Most would probably say no. I understand that this type of chink in the armor of your discipline may be troublesome to you, but you may find that people respond better to your overall discipline routine if you are reasonable in what you consider a breach of discipline. If this is not your problem, then I have the following second question for you: How are you disciplining the students? Do you have a routine procedure in which you calmly, and with little classroom disruption, inform students of their infractions and their consequences, or do you berate or belittle students and take up lots of class time dealing with infractions and lectures about how you will not tolerate misbehavior? If this is the case, you are putting yourself at risk for reprimands that could be placed in your personnel file as well as incurring the protests of students and parents. Listen to what the parents and students are saying and see if it has merit. If you believe it does not, ask some of your peers to observe your class and give their opinions. A fair but firm teacher usually does not elicit openly belligerent students and parents.

I am a very emotional person, and I tend to take misbehavior as a personal insult. When I explain to students how they make me feel and how they hurt my feelings, they smile and say that they are sorry, but then they do the behavior again! Why don't students have more respect for me and my feelings?

You are an authority figure. Whether you were their teacher or someone else, the same students would engage in the same misbehavior. It is nothing personal! These students do not even know you as a person; you are merely their teacher, and therefore they will misbehave. Frankly, the minute you start talking about your feelings, the students may smile politely, but behind your back you are becoming a laughing stock and labeled as a teacher who can be "got." They do not care about your feelings; they care about what you can do to them. Get tough and get off the emotional ride you are allowing your students to place you on. Why are you letting children dictate how you feel? Lay down the law, state the rules and consequences, and enforce them calmly and dispassionately. Do you think policemen get personally upset when someone engages in a crime? No way! Neither should you. What should concern you is removing or controlling the bad, disrespectful influences in your classroom who are inhibiting the behaving students from learning. That is your job, and you need to get it in hand before you lose control of all your students and, hence, all your teaching.

Chapter 5

ↄ✖ↄ

"What Do You Mean, 'How Will You Use This In the Real World?' This *Is* the Real World!"

Helping Students Succeed

What does it take for a student to succeed in school? Is it just intelligence alone, or is it also motivation, good organizational skills, responsible behavior, the ability to take good notes, the ability to connect knowledge across disciplines, and the knowledge of how to study for and take tests? Most teachers would say that these are some of the prerequisites for learning almost any subject. Now more than ever, a large part of our job as teachers is to teach these skills in addition to math, languages, and history. As the pressure continues to mount for students to succeed in grades, test scores, extracurricular activities, and other personal achievements, the need for teachers to address all aspects of student success also increases. One of the most important questions a teacher will ever face is how to help students reach their greatest potential. Only a few of the solutions are presented in this chapter, with the hope that even more answers can be generated.

My students seem to lack any intellectual curiosity. They simply accept what I tell them as fact without questioning it. How can I get them to ask intelligent questions and actively seek knowledge rather than passively receiving it?

Many students have been trained by years of lecture and drill to passively accept knowledge. You need to train them in how to ask questions and how to be active participants in their own learning. To do this, you need to model appropriate behavior. Sometimes teachers tend to rush to supply answers when students have questions or difficulty in understanding. Ideally, the intellectual struggle should be encouraged, and teachers should function as guides in the questioning process. You should ask leading questions and encourage students to seek alternative explanations and answers. Do not rush to answer students questions but, rather, ask further questions of the students that will let them discover the answers on their own. Allow students to debate points or take over the teaching of different concepts, particularly if you have failed to get the idea across. Essentially, you will be teaching your students how to learn as well as teaching the content.

Intellectual curiosity can also be heightened through motivating students to want to learn about the subject. Some teachers use a KWL chart to start off a new topic. *KWL* is an acronym for "what you know, what you want to know, and what you learned." Students are asked to identify what they currently know about a topic, what they wish they knew, and after instruction, what they learned. This works well for all grades. Other teachers motivate students to learn through bringing in interesting guest speakers related to the topic that they are teaching. Field trips also motivate students, especially if they are required to use all of their senses to explore their surroundings and relate it back to their school work. Whatever you find that makes your students want to learn for learning sake, not just for a grade, will increase their capacity for intellectual curiosity.

I have several students who do all their homework, participate in all the labs, answer all the questions in class, and seem to know all the material during class exercises. Yet without fail, these students do poorly on written tests and quizzes. What is going on?

This is a very common question and one that plagues every teacher who has been confronted by an expectant parent waiting for a diagnosis of why their hard-working child is failing the class. The best place to start looking for the answers is the students themselves. Ask leading questions regarding issues such as how much time is spent studying daily versus the amount of time spent cramming before tests. Is there a feeling of great anxiety when confronted with a test that causes mental blocks? Does the student feel rushed and in need of more time? Would it help if either the questions or answers were given orally? If the answers to these types of questions do not hold the key to the poor performance, examine the student's notebook and check for problems with organization or handwriting and clues for dyslexia and other learning disorders. If this is also satisfactory, check with the child's other teachers to see if similar problems are occurring or is it just in your class. If this is just your class, could it be a personality clash, a dislike of the subject, peer pressure within that class, or some other emotional factor? If all of this still gives you no clue to the poor performance, you may need to refer the child to a guidance counselor, school psychologist, or learning disabilities specialist to make a more clinical diagnosis. However, most times the answer is fairly easy to uncover if you probe the situation carefully.

My students have the attention span of a very young gnat. After 10 minutes of class, everyone starts to fidget, and discipline goes out the window. Nobody is paying any attention to me! What can I do to keep them on task?

First, read Chapter 1 about getting students to respect you. Second, do not fight this battle by trying to maintain firm discipline; you will never get any teaching done. For whatever reason—immaturity, lack of interest, or a sugar-high from lunch—these kids are unable to concentrate for long periods of time. Therefore, it is your job to develop teaching strategies to meet them on their level. Break your instructional time into small increments. For example, have an interesting puzzle or question posted on the board that they can work on answering even before class starts. Give a reward of some sort for the correct answer to foster competition. Lecture for 10 minutes, and then let students discuss the lecture with each other for 10 minutes. Also, you may give them group work to practice and let different groups present their findings. You may also do a project that requires the students to get up and walk around the room (or the school) to complete it and then culminate with another review and possibly more rewards. Frankly, this is a great idea for all classes because even though discipline may not always go out the window, most of their minds have flown the coop midway through the lecture anyway. It is hard to listen to other people talk at you all day long. Make it a little more interesting and a lot heavier on student involvement.

This is probably a common complaint of high school teachers, but my freshmen students seem to be totally new to the idea of taking notes and being responsible for their own work. What are they doing to them down in middle school? I cannot hold their hands through the whole year!

Shame, shame, shame! It is hard enough to teach without having your colleagues downgrade what you are doing. Middle school teachers deserve a special place in heaven. If you think they are doing something different from the high school teachers, you are right. What is appropriate in middle school is only somewhat appropriate in high school. If you recognize that freshmen students have not grasped the idea of taking notes and organizing their own notebooks and projects, then why don't you teach them? And if you do not have the time, get your administration to offer summer preparation courses or pull-out time in the beginning of the school year to train these kids. Perhaps your administration can even coordinate with the middle schools to offer short courses in this very topic. There is plenty of material available out there on how to take notes and organize. As far as being responsible for their own work, that is something that comes with maturity and experiencing the consequences of not being responsible for themselves. Emphasize to your students that you expect them to be responsible for missed assignments, making up work, and so forth. After a few times of dealing with the negative results of irresponsibility, students usually wise up. Be gentle with your freshmen and give them a little time to learn more than just the three Rs.

❧

I plan my lessons very carefully, with a lot of demonstration and explanation. Yet my students still cannot seem to retain the information. What can I do to get them to remember their lessons?

❧

There are two major tactics that will work for this. First, I am sure you have seen the old pyramid showing the degree of learning that takes place with lecture versus hands-on practice versus teaching others. Lecture alone produces the least amount of retention. More retention is achieved when students are actively or physically involved in the learning process, and even more is achieved when students have to teach others. Remember the following old proverb: "If I hear, I forget; If I see, I remember; If I do, I understand." Incorporate these ideas in your lessons, and you should see retention improve. A second tactic is review, review, and review. Review at the start of class, have students recite key points to each other during class, require students to write major points of the lesson to be allowed to leave the class, review at the end of class by asking questions, and then do it all over again the next day. Plan whole days where you do nothing but review the work for the past month. Also, do incremental reviews by putting questions from Chapter 1 on a test for Chapter 4 so that the students have to remember the material. You should remember that meaningful repetition leads to retention.

❧

Many of my students say that they need extra help outside of regular class. How can I accommodate 150 students' requests and still have a life?

❧

Individual tutoring is a big part of the demands on a teacher's time. Try to get as much of the tutoring done during the class day (breaks, lunch, briefly after or before school, etc.) as possible. Have times posted when you will be available, and let students sign up for an appointment for the block of time you deem appropriate. You may also offer group tutoring in different subjects on different days of the week. Do not overload yourself, however, so that you have no spare time in the day. If a student needs more than you can deliver, offer alternative routes to the student. Keep a roster of competent students who would be willing to tutor others for small amounts of hourly pay. If peer tutoring will not work (and sometimes it does not), check with your guidance department for names of professional tutors. As of this writing, an adult tutor may charge from $20 to $35 per hour and may or may not come to the student's home. Also, you might find out if it is possible to have a teachers' aide or parent volunteer help students individually during class. Before you get into all this tutoring business, you may want to encourage the students to seek help during class. Often, tutoring is unnecessary if students just speak up and ask questions during class time. In fact, read the next question and answer that addresses this very issue.

❧

When I ask if there are any questions in class, there is dead silence. Yet during tutoring, students tell me that they had questions on a variety of topics. What gives?

❧

Students are afraid to ask questions in class for many reasons, not the least of which is fear of being thought stupid by their peers or teachers. Some of it is just shyness or the attitude of "I'll figure it out myself!" You need to actively promote a class atmosphere conducive to asking questions. This can be done by constantly scanning the faces of your students, looking for the ones who look more puzzled than others and asking them if they have questions. Large displays with slogans (e.g., "There is no such thing as a stupid question" "The only thing that is stupid is not asking a question") tend to keep the issue in the forefronts of their minds. Reinforce question asking by praising good questions for their intelligence, insight, or importance. Model the behavior you want by constantly asking lots of probing questions directed to both the class as a whole and individual students. (Helpful hint: Ask questions first, and then call on a particular student. It keeps everyone more alert!) Above all, never, under any circumstances, ridicule a child for asking a legitimate question, even if you have already given the answer to it 12 times in the past half hour. This is a sure way to bring all questions to a screeching halt for the rest of the year.

When a student does badly on a test, should I let him or her retake it? Should it be a policy of mine to let all students make up quizzes or tests on which they fail?

Theoretically, it makes a lot of sense to have students retake different versions of tests they failed. After all, we want them to learn the material before going forward as well as give them a chance to show that they have mastered the material. Many educational theories espouse the positive aspects of this policy. However, I have never met a teacher who had it work in reality.

What usually happens is students feel the first test you give them is the *practice* test, and when they fail it or wish to make a higher grade, then they will take the *real* test. This means that you end up making many versions of the same test, scheduling innumerable makeup sessions for students, and grading two to three times as many papers as you normally would. One way to give students multiple chances to learn material and demonstrate their mastery is by the use of multiple quizzes within a unit, perhaps with the policy of dropping the lowest one, and then a cumulative test for the unit. This gives the students many ways to demonstrate mastery without your having to redo your tests and grades multiple times.

What should be my policy if students do not finish a test within the allotted time period? Do I have to let them have more time?

This is really subject to your own discretion and knowledge of your students. I have had many students who work slowly and methodically, and given ample time, they will perform well on tests. Some students have disabilities that require them to have additional time. However, some students do not finish a test on purpose so that they can go away and look up the answers or converse with their friends and come back and finish with renewed knowledge at a later time. Unless you know the student well and can personally vouch for his or her need for extra time, look at the student's tests to see if whether it is only one or two questions that he or she needs to finish or most of the test. If only a few questions remain to be answered, see if the student can stay a little later in your class and be late to their next one. If there is a lot of blank space left in the test, circle those unanswered questions and do not accept changes to any other questions. Grade the questions that are already finished, if you can, before the student comes back to finish the others. If most of the test is unfinished, ask the student why he or she did not take time during class to do the test and judge whether you will let the student finish. Of course, it is always within your power to simply say, "Time is up." I have found that by doing this, students tend to get finished with the work on time. Amazing, isn't it?

My students seem unable to connect pieces of information to each other. They learn everything as separate units of knowledge that are unrelated to anything else. How can I get them to learn to connect their learning to build a unified whole?

Part of your job as a teacher is to guarantee that learning is a connective process and that your subject matter is integrated not only with what precedes and succeeds your current unit but also is integrated with other subjects. I suggest that you give kids a visual framework for every unit that shows how it is connected with other units in the grand scheme of your yearly course. This could be an outline, note sheet, or some type of graphic organizer such as a flowchart, bulletin board, wall poster, or other exhibit. These pictures show the relative importance of concepts in your own particular subject. Always give your students the big picture before you have them learn the details. To integrate your subject with others, borrow this idea from many middle school teachers; meet regularly to coordinate your units with those of teachers of other disciplines to determine how you can tie in your subject with their subjects. For example, perhaps your math students are studying the equation of a line. They might benefit from the psychology teacher's demonstration of regression lines used in analyzing collected data, from the economics teacher's explanation of elementary cost function graphs, or from the mechanical drawing teacher's exhibition of the use of slope in mechanical designs. You might also try inviting guest speakers who use the material you are teaching in real-life occupations. Regardless of how you do the integrating, just remember that it is your job to do it; after all, you know better than any of your students how your subject fits in the grand scheme of things. Just be sure you let them know as well.

What is the best way to give encouragement to kids who seem to fail at every task I give them? How can I persuade them to keep trying and not give up?

First, let students know that you really care about their progress. One of the best ways to do this is to talk to them individually and ask them what they feel the problem is and what you can do to help them. Then, set goals with them. For example, on the next quiz, instead of trying for a 100%, tell them to try for a 70% instead. When they meet it, reward them with praise, stickers, candy, or something else that is meaningful for them. Perhaps you could call their parents to give them the good news. After they have reached this goal, raise it. You may also include other goals in your contract with these students such as doing 100% of homework, asking two questions per class each day, volunteering to work one problem per week in front of the class, and so forth. By establishing small, achievable goals, students can see that they are making progress at each step instead of seeing only the large failures.

I am starting to think that if I only knew more about my students personally, I could teach them better. What are some good ways to learn about students' personal lives without being too intrusive?

You can easily learn about the academic history of your students by studying their student records and standardized test scores as well as by talking to other teachers at your school who have taught or are teaching your students. There may be a master list at your school that shows membership in each club and sport so you can check your students for their extracurricular interests. As for their personal lives, elementary school students usually enjoy sharing this information through pictures of their family and pets and show-and-tell activities. High school students like to write about themselves, and much information can be gleaned from this. If you wish to know more, ask the guidance office, which generally has knowledge of the particulars of students' personal lives. The school nurse can inform you of any illnesses or conditions students may have. The one place you do not want to go for information is the students' friends, for obvious reasons, and you probably do not want to ask the students or their parents directly either. If you are gifted at the art of steering conversations in the direction you wish them to go, by all means talk to the parents of the student. But frankly, it is often best to stick to information you can obtain through the school itself.

Sometimes I feel that I have explained things until I am totally exasperated! I try three or four ways to explain a concept and students still do not get it! I finally just give

up and move on. How can I get across a concept to kids
when I have exhausted every method I know to teach it?

First of all, try to be sure that they are truly not understanding the
concepts and not just trying to frustrate you! One way to do this
is to quiz students in depth about the nature of their questions to
probe their misunderstandings. If they back off, they were just
playing with you. If they answer, then you have a good chance to
diagnose their problems. If in-depth questioning does not solve
their problems, try letting other students who seem to understand come to the front of the class and try to explain the concepts. This usually works well. Locate videotapes or software
that explain the same ideas. Ask other teachers who teach the
same subject how they approached these types of concepts.
Above all, do not get frustrated. If the students really do not
understand and the tension level in the room is getting high, back
off and simply tell them that you will try and think of another
approach to the concept for tomorrow. In the meantime, review
past work, work simpler problems they understand, or do something constructive that diffuses their tension and yours until you
can come up with some different way to approach the concept.

I have several students with severe cases of test anxiety.
It is so bad that it will probably affect their ability to get
into college and pursue the careers they want. What can
I do to help these kids succeed on their tests?

Talk to the kids individually to determine the nature of their
problem. Do they have a learning disability you do not know

about, is there a physical problem such as bad eyesight or hearing, or is it really that the students get so nervous that they freeze? If being nervous is their problem, quiz the kids about how much they study and when. It may simply be a case of their knowing they are not well prepared and reacting understandably to this. If the students do seem to be preparing for the tests in a reasonable fashion and are still getting terribly nervous, then it seems you do have a true case of test anxiety on your hands. If you can, try to accommodate them in ways that may relieve their nervousness. I have given tests one-on-one to students, orally and written, and this often seems to help. Sometimes, additional time made available to the students (e.g., after class or during lunch periods) seems to ease their anxiety about having enough time to finish or check their work. If you absolutely cannot make accommodations for the students, then set up a meeting with their parents and their guidance counselor or some other individual skilled in handling test anxiety to work out a solution that is mutually agreeable. You are to be commended that you take this so seriously. Test anxiety is a real feeling and can be a tremendous detriment to people who suffer from it.

I do many recommendations for kids to go to college, get jobs, and so forth. Once in a while, students ask me to do recommendations for them when I do not really feel that I can recommend them. I do not want to stop them from pursuing their goals and helping them succeed, but, in good conscience, I cannot recommend them. What do I do in this situation?

Be up front with students and do not accept the inevitable forms they shove in your hands on their way out your door. Simply tell them that you believe they should ask someone else because your recommendation may not be as good as they would like. If they ask why, say that their grades, attitude, or some other factor keeps you from giving them a top recommendation. If you have a very sticky situation in which you do not feel you could be straightforward with the student for whatever reason, then a little white lie will suffice. Try an answer such as, "I really don't have the time to do anymore recommendations right now. I have too much paperwork to do as it is. Sorry!" It works!

CHAPTER
⊷⊶ **6**

PARENTS ARE OUR FRIENDS ... WELL, MOSTLY

Dealing With Parents

Parents can be a teacher's greatest ally and support. The parent-teacher team is a powerful combination in helping students to succeed. Parents are also an invaluable source of information for the best method of instructing or disciplining their children and can make your job much easier on a daily basis. Parents can also be fabulous resources, giving of their time and knowledge to aid you in your quest to be a great teacher for their children. Supportive, concerned, caring, and involved parents are one of a teacher's best assets. However, every now and then a parent comes along who makes you appreciate all the other parents even more. This is the unreasonable, illogical, belligerent, antagonistic parent that causes you to think that hospitalization would be a better alternative than having a parent conference with him or her. How do you deal with this type of parent and still keep your temper, not to mention your sanity? A few ideas are presented in this chapter.

Communication

> I have 155 students and am on five committees and two
> evaluation teams. I sponsor two clubs and am required
> by my district to attend special training for one of the
> courses I teach. I have 1 hour of planning available to me
> each day. Yet I am dealing with several irate parents who
> think that monthly progress reports and attendance cards
> are inadequate and who want me to call them each time
> their child does not take notes, has no materials, does not
> turn in homework, and so on. These parents think I work
> for them and phone my principal and folks at the district
> office to complain about why they do not get adequate
> information! I have asked them to call me, as it would
> seem easier, but they do not see it that way! What do you
> do with unreasonable demands by vocal and obnoxious
> parents?

Unfortunately, unreasonable and obnoxious parents tend to
get even more unreasonable and obnoxious unless they are
appeased in some fashion. The trick is to appease them in the
least time-consuming way as well as to provide a paper trail for
yourself that proves you have tried to cooperate with them. In
addition to all else you send home, inform parents that students
can pick up forms from you once a week that will detail grades
for the week, whether homework was turned in, behavior, attendance, upcoming tests and projects, and so forth. Tell them that
it is the student's responsibility to request these forms and bring
them home to the parent, not the teacher's. If parents do not
receive a form on the designated day, then they know there is a
problem with the student and they should call for information.
This puts the burden on both the student *and* the parent to keep

track of their progress and *not* on you. Remember to make the form easy to fill out, and have a lot of copies handy. Take time to copy each completed form as added proof that you have tried to communicate with parents. Take this opportunity to remind the parent how to contact you by phone, e-mail, voice mail, or regular mail. Perhaps some kind of system can be worked out in which both the parent and the teacher can accommodate each other within their own time frames.

At the beginning of every school year, I have a number of parents who ask for my home phone number "just in case" they want to call me about their child or if their child needs help doing their homework at night. Is this a good practice? I will have no life if I am on the phone all night helping kids do their homework!

This is not a good practice! You are not "on call" for your students 24 hours a day, unless you really want to be, which most of us do not! When parents ask for that information, simply say, "I don't give out my home phone. I am sure you understand that I have 160 students, and it is impossible to be on-call for all of them at every hour of day. Please feel free to call me at school, and I will be happy to return your call. Also, I offer extra help for students at lunch/after school/on Wednesdays." Most parents will understand when you phrase it this way. You are under no obligation to give out your personal information to anyone at any time!

I give 200% every day on the job, and yet I have parents who prefer me to return their calls at their convenience.

The last parent wanted me to return her call between 8:30 p.m. and 8:45 p.m. so that she would not miss her favorite television show! What do you do with parents who think a teacher's workday has no end?

Some parents think that teachers work only for them because we have their child in our class. Most teachers are occupied with their own lives at night and truthfully cannot talk to parents because they have no time. Simply call those parents who request unreasonable times for a callback at their work during normal business hours and state your policy of not returning phone calls after 4:00 p.m. If this does not meet their needs, ask them to put the requested information in writing, either postal or e-mail, and you will respond in kind. No one can reasonably require you to call these parents on your own time.

I am getting afraid to write any negative comments or even send home bad grades. I just learned that one of my students has a father who mentally abuses her and punishes her severely if she receives negative comments from her teachers. It is not physical abuse, but the kid is miserable and deathly afraid of anything negative being sent home. What should I do?

If you ever suspect physical abuse, you are under legal obligation to report it to your department of social services immediately. By not doing so, you put yourself in jeopardy of legal action as well as putting the child in continued peril. You are caught in a bad situation. If you do not send any information home and the child gets Fs on report cards, not only will the parent abuse the child for the bad grades but also the parent will in turn haul you up in front of your principal for failing to notify him earlier of his or her child's lack of progress. If you do send information home, then as you said, you risk putting the child in jeopardy. It is doubtful that this particular child ever misbehaves in class, knowing that the punishment he or she will receive at home would be far worse than anything the teacher could devise. On the other hand, some students tend to act out when they are in this kind of situation. If it is a behavior problem, try to deal with it in class without involving the parent. If the grades are good, then you do not need to worry about contacting the parent; if the grades are bad, then you really should notify the parent. Try sending home lots of positive comments about the child to counterbalance the bad grades. Because this is a difficult situation, you should seek assistance from your administration or guidance department. They often have information that you do not.

Everything I tell one of my student's parent is totally wrong, according to the parent. If I say that in my professional opinion, this or that should be done, he says that it will not work. If I try to tell him what is going on in the class, he says it is not the way it seems. I am totally frustrated and out of ideas as to how to deal with this man. What should I do?

Do not be frustrated, just do not talk to him in person. You will not accomplish anything anyway. Send all of your information and ideas to him in writing and keep copies for yourself. This way you are assured that he is getting the information, he cannot complain about a lack of communication later, and whether he

chooses to accept your opinions and ideas is solely up to
him. If he calls you, calmly restate your position and ideas.
When he says they do not work, ask him what he thinks should
be done. At least that puts the burden on him to come up with
some solutions.

How can you involve parents if they will not speak to
you? Literally? I just got off the phone with a mother who
said "hello" at the beginning of the call, grunted twice
during the call, and then hung up without saying good-
bye! At one point, I asked, "Are you still there?" and that
was when I received one of the grunts. What should I do
next? I obviously can expect nothing from her!

At least you know more about what the child is dealing with at
home! Obviously, you cannot expect help at all from this mother.
Perhaps the father could be more helpful. If not, then you need
to devise ways to help the situation yourself, whether it is disciplining the child consistently, tutoring the child, or involving
counselors, school psychologists, or social workers. Keep the
parents informed periodically through written correspondence
and keep a copy for yourself. You might also want to document
the unresponsive nature of the parent and have the guidance
office keep a copy in their file on that student. It could help other
teachers who have to deal with the student.

I have a parent who refuses to talk to me; she constantly
goes over my head to assistant principals, principals, and
in one case, even the district office! Why can't she come

to me with her concerns about her child? All she wanted to know was how the child could make up work, how to get extra help, and other such routine questions. Nothing unusual is going on with her child, it is just the parent's inability to talk directly to me! The people she called ended up calling me asking for the information and relaying it back to her. I feel it makes me look like some uncommunicative monster. What can I do to change this situation?

She should have received a copy of your rules and policies for routine matters at the beginning of school. Send her another copy. Tell the administrators and folks at the district office how you feel about being out of the communication loop and that you are wondering why she will not contact you personally. This puts the question in the minds of the administrators regarding her, not you. Ask them to tell her to phone you directly at school so that you can answer her questions, and if she will not do that, ask the administrators to inquire why so that you will know what is going on. Maybe it is just a simple matter of her having trouble reaching you during the day because you are in class, and it is easier for her to reach people who work in their offices. If you like, why don't you phone her occasionally with good news about her child so that she gets accustomed to talking to you? Stress the fact that she is welcome to contact you at any time, and you will be happy to return her call or email at any time. If she still refuses to contact you, chalk it up to another strange parent and continue answering her questions through third parties. Send home periodic written progress reports, very short and informal, to show that you attempted to communicate directly with her.

This is kind of unusual, but I have a parent who exaggerates everything. If her child missed two homework assignments, she gets hysterical and screams at him for never doing any homework. If he fails a quiz, the mother schedules a teacher conference with the guidance office and the assistant principal to discuss why her child is flunking out of school! She is a real problem in that you can never take what she says at face value. I am always afraid she is going to cause yet another big commotion. What can I do to somewhat tone her down?

You really cannot affect her behavior too much; you just have to deal with the outcome of it. She is making herself known to be a hysterical person that no one wants to deal with. She is another parent with whom you should avoid personal contact and communicate only in written fashion. Not only does this serve the purpose of keeping her informed but it also allows involved parties to refer to what was actually being said rather than her overblown version of it. If you must meet with her in person, arrange to have a witness present. Try to avoid letting her rant and rave by being well prepared with descriptions of the problems (if any), the lack of problems (more likely), possible solutions, and the actions you believe she or her child should take. Do not give her a chance to throw a tantrum. Just state your case, stand up and extend your hand, and excuse yourself. You do not have enough time in the day to deal with parental outbursts!

What do you do with parents who make nuisances of themselves? I have one parent who calls at least twice a week, comes by the school several times in a month, pops in unannounced to see the principal to discuss how the teachers are doing their jobs, requests conferences once a month, and so on. He even wants my home number so that he can discuss his child when it is more convenient for him! Everybody at school cringes when they see him coming. His child is very normal, average grades, and not a problem. So what is the consuming interest in bugging everyone to death?

Although this type of parent is annoying, there are two good sides to him. First, he can never claim that he has not received enough information about his child, and you do not have to make any special effort to get it to him. Second, he really is a concerned parent, so why don't you turn the situation around to your advantage? Say to him, "I am delighted you are so involved in your child's education. We need more parents like you. Because you are so interested and involved, maybe you could help me out? I need [insert a request here such as guest speakers, chaperones, class assistance, someone to copy handouts, tutors, transportation, money, computers, whatever]. I know you want your child to have the best education possible and this would really help!" If you do this, either the parent will come through and be a benefit to you or he will try to avoid you so that you do not ask him to do anything else. Either way, you win!

PARENT CONFERENCES

Sometimes when I go into parent conferences, parents feel compelled to give me the entire family history! They go into their child's infancy practically, even though I am a high school teacher. Sometimes they mention siblings that I do not even know. I would not mind if it somehow all tied together and helped me figure out the basic problems that their students are having, but most of the time it seems like just rambling, and the clock ticks by and nothing is resolved. How can I meet with parents so that I avoid this, resolve everyone's problems, and still leave school at a reasonable hour?

First of all, have some sympathy. These are concerned and worried parents, and concerned and worried people tend to ramble nervously. You, as the cool professional that you are, need to focus on the issues. Listen sympathetically for a few minutes and when you see there is no hope of the parent coming to the point in the next 5 hours, try to get a word in edgewise. Say something such as the following:

> I know it is so tough being a parent and I am happy you came in today. Johnny seems to be having trouble with [insert problem here]. Here are some things I think might help [insert solutions here]. If you would just make sure that [insert what you want the parent and/or the student to do here]. Does that sound workable to you?

Sometimes parents will agree and yet continue to ramble on about their children's past. Again, listen sympathetically for a few minutes and then interject, "I understand. But I think we have come up with some workable solutions to the problem today, and I am hopeful that things will be better. Please feel free to call me at school anytime you have concerns. Thanks so much for coming in today!" Then stand up and shake hands at this point so that they get the hint. You may wish to follow up with a written synopsis of what occured in the meeting and what outcomes have occurred since then. This sounds cold, but in reality you have accomplished the objective of the meeting and have communicated with the parent clearly and efficiently. What more could you want?

I am beginning to hate having parent conferences in which parents bring their children with them. Half the time, these parents embarrass their kids by revealing things the students surely would not want their teacher to know. One time, I had both parents yelling into each ear of one poor boy simultaneously for 5 solid minutes. The kid was miserable, I was embarrassed, and nothing got accomplished. What should I do? Refuse to meet with the parent if the child is there?

It is often a good idea to have the child present at a parent conference because, after all, the conference is about the child! Together, the parent and teacher can present a united front and the child is usually unwilling to disagree with the teacher's assessment of his or her progress or behavior if the teacher is sitting there. However, this can also backfire if the parent and child take sides against the teacher, or if, as you describe, the parent decides this is a great time to embarrass and berate his or her child. As far as you are concerned professionally, having parents scream at their children is a waste of your time and accomplishes nothing. If you see this is the direction the conference is heading, you need to interject yourself into it. Speak directly to the child first, stating what you would like to talk to his or her parent about, and ask the child if he or she would mind stepping outside the door for a few minutes. Most kids will be delighted to leave the situation, and if the parent objects, simply restate your position that you really need to speak with the parent privately and that you will bring the child back to the conference in a few minutes. It will be a rare parent who will continue to disagree with this. Once the child leaves, turn to the parent, state the problem, your possible solutions, and what you want the parent to do. Do not give the parent a chance to get on a tirade about how awful his or her child is. However, you should ask the parent if he or she has any questions or comments after you finish your speech. If the parent tries to stray from the subject again, simply restate what you wish him or her to do and suggest that the child come back to learn the outcome of your conversation. At this point, you must beat the parent to the first word. If you can, you will be able to explain to the child clearly and quickly what you and the parent discussed and the agreed solutions. Tell the child that you expect a change the next time you see him or her in class. Then turn quickly to the parent, stand up, thank him or her for the conference, and extend your hand. This may sound fairly cold, but again, it does no one any good to embarrass children and their teachers by letting parents yell about their children's supposed shortcomings.

I have just had a parent conference out of the twilight zone. The mother claims she was admitted to the emergency room twice for stress-related illnesses caused by her child's grades, and now she is threatening a lawsuit because of the conspiracy of teachers against her child! The kid is sweet and tries hard, but he has a bizarre parent that I will have to deal with all year. What should I do?

Most parents are nice, normal people, but occasionally you will run into some that are really bizarre. Try to appease this woman as much as you can. Supply her with whatever she wants as long as it is within reason and you wish to do it. Call her occasionally just to reinforce the good things that are going on. This is a really big help in dealing with a parent who is essentially hysterical because it calms them. Alert your guidance office and administration about this strange parental behavior before they encounter a surprise visit from this woman. They may have some insider information about this parent you need to know. Above all, avoid meeting this woman without having a witness present, preferably a counselor or administrator. Keep track of all you do for her and the times you call her, just in case she decides to do something ridiculous legally and finds a lawyer willing to believe her. It does happen, unfortunately! Try to remember that this student is sweet and is not responsible for his weird parent, so do not take it out on him.

I just met with a mother who seems afraid of her own son. During the conference, he threatened her and even drew back his hand as if to hit her. She flinched and tearfully continued the conference. The boy is manageable in my classroom but seems to be about to blow at any given time. How can I deal with this situation in terms of parental involvement when I am afraid of what awaits the mother at home?

You must realize that parental involvement from the mother in this case is impossible. The parent is afraid of her own son, so discipline and guidance from her will be unlikely. Continue doing whatever you have to do to keep the boy manageable, but alert the school social worker, psychologist, and principal of the situation, preferably in writing. Do not let the boy know that you have done this, and be sure that no one else tells him. However, the situation will be documented in case you or the mother need it later. Furthermore, you will have records that you requested assistance, just in case.

❦

I thought parents were supposed to be our allies, but in a recent conference, a set of parents sat there and defended their child's right to wear obscene shirts to school (freedom of expression), their child's nonexistent homework (I assign too much for anybody to do), and their child's cheating (I made it too easy for him to do so). How can I answer charges like these while trying to get some sort of help with a very difficult child?

❦

This is one of the hardest situations for teachers because you cannot expect help at all from the parents, and the child gets the message that his behavior is OK with mom and dad and you are the one who is wrong. It is no wonder that the child is very difficult. All you can really do is discipline the child consistently and require him to do all the academic work that the other children do. Follow school procedures regarding cheating, dress code, and so forth and be sure he is punished accordingly. Document this conference and file it in the guidance office in the student's folder. Send a copy to the office for the principal's files as well. State that because of their belligerent attitude, you believe no further personal contact with the parents will be beneficial. Send home all routine reports and, if you like, send home periodic written notifications of behavior and academic progress, but do not attempt to contact these people personally again. If, for some reason, you must meet with them, request that a witness be present.

7

TELL ME AGAIN, HOW LONG HAS IT BEEN SINCE YOU TAUGHT?

Dealing With Administrators

Good administrators are worth their weight in gold. They can be your source of support, your advocate in times of difficulty, your main cheerleader, and your friend and colleague. An efficient, orderly school full of caring and concerned professionals is not an accident; much credit goes to the administrators. Being an excellent principal or assistant principal requires an extensive knowledge of all facets of education, the ability to make correct decisions quickly, extreme diplomacy, a genuine desire to work with people and empathize with their problems, and, above all, outstanding communication skills. What an ideal educational world it would be if all administrators possessed these traits! However, it is not an ideal world and at some point in their careers, teachers may encounter some principals or assistant principals who have less than desirable characteristics.

Teaching is a difficult enough endeavor without having to be at odds with the administration. The following unfortunate experiences may provide some ideas about how to handle this most upsetting and frustrating aspect of teaching if it occurs during your career.

MANAGEMENT ISSUES

We just got a new principal and some new assistant principals at our school. This is the first year in their current leadership positions for all of them. There is lots of confusion and nobody seems to know what is going on, except for us teachers who have worked here for a while. How can we give input and guidance to this group without seeming to be overbearing, nosy, know-it-alls?

You will not seem that way at all if you approach the situation correctly. Schedule meetings between representatives from each department or grade level and the new administration. The topics of the meetings should include an introduction to the teachers and their respective styles, issues for each department or grade, problems and successes for each as well as solutions that each department or grade level would like to see implemented, and an offer of support and assistance with the new transition. There is certainly nothing wrong with this approach, and in fact, it would be welcomed by most reasonable administrators. The faculty really needs to take a proactive approach because if the cooler heads do not prevail and make themselves known, then the hotheads on your faculty will do the job for you and misrepresent the school and various persons in it. You really do not want tattletales, naysayers, and the pessimistic gloom-and-doom set to be tugging on the ears of your new administration. They might get depressed and quit, or unfortunately, they might see these types of people as their true friends in their new position and take their words as truth. So quit worrying about the impression you will make and get organized to actively make a good impression.

The administration at my school believes in visiting teacher classrooms too often, in my opinion. Not only do the administrators visit but also I have visiting students from other schools who want to check out our school, visiting students from other countries who want to learn about the American classroom, student teachers, interning teachers, educational students who observe, groups of teachers from other schools, university professors, and even parents and business groups at times. I am amazed on days when it is just me and my class! Can I ever lock the door and say, "No one but students allowed"?

Let's take each group separately. First of all, be thankful your administration cares enough to set foot in your classroom frequently. This makes it much easier for the quality of your daily work to speak for itself instead of a brief evaluation every year. It also makes the administration more likely to support you with materials, assistants, or whatever you need to continue your excellent work. As far as students visiting from other schools just to check out your school, most schools allow teachers to refuse these students, particularly if they cause disruptions. Students from other countries are usually welcome additions to your classroom because they are typically excellent students who try very hard. In addition, you will find out a lot of information about what education is like in other countries, and that is very interesting. As for student teachers, interning teachers, and educational students who observe, you are usually free to deny them admittance to your classroom. However, a good student teacher is an excellent perk for a busy classroom teacher. Even student teachers who need a little more help can be very rewarding. Besides, professional teachers have a responsibility to help prepare future teachers when they can. It is a professional courtesy to allow groups of teachers from other schools to observe. If you have a chance to speak with them (e.g., over lunch), you may find out practices they have in place at their school that will be of particular use or interest to you or your school. University professors are typically great fun to have in your class because they are so sympathetic to what you must deal with every day. They also are good resources to have in case you need something such as guest lecturers, grant money, or access to something at the university. As far as parents and business groups visiting classes, this could be either good or bad, but it is not in your best interests to say no to this because it looks like you are trying to hide something. It is easy to get tired of this endless parade of people in your classroom, but look at it this way: If you were a really bad teacher, you would not be on display like this, so in a way it is a compliment!

My principal is so busy with the detail work of the school that she fails to have any kind of vision for where we are headed. I understand that she has got a lot to do, but where is the kind of educational leadership we are supposed to have and how can we get it at my school?

This is now an unfortunate fact of life in most schools. It is a rare administrator who actually has the time to visit classrooms frequently, patrol the halls, talk casually with students and teachers, and oversee curriculum and learning-related issues. Today's administrators are busy dealing with potential lawsuits, police reports, drug raids, personnel problems, dilapidated buildings, increased accountability reports, formal evaluations, and so forth. If they have time to provide educational leadership and a vision for the school, they are rare indeed. If your administrator is finding it difficult, then the faculty may have to define it. If necessary, make an overt request to the principal for faculty time to meet and discuss a vision for the educational future of their school. Continue to involve more and more faculty members until you decide what is going to be the standard at your school. Your principal will welcome the help and praise your initiative, assuming that he or she is a reasonable person. (Unreasonable administrators are dealt with in later questions.) An added benefit is that this kind of concern for a school's well-being and the subsequent action on behalf of the school will put you in a very positive limelight from both the district and community standpoint.

I feel very intimidated by my principal and one of my assistant principals. They use a lot of veiled threats and half-statements so that I am never sure what is going on or what they really think of me. I have talked with other teachers at my school and this seems to be happening to them as well. Our faculty feels totally out of the loop as far as the direction of the school goes and is frankly too intimidated to demand a change. We feel as if we are always in some kind of trouble, but we never know for what! What should we do?

Administration by intimidation is something that has caused many good teachers to transfer or to quit the business altogether.

If you are in this situation, your faculty meetings consist of a lot of accusations: "Some of you are engaging in [this behavior or that behavior] and we know who you are! We are watching, and we will take action!" Sound familiar? All the good folks who are not doing anything wrong feel like they are being wrongly accused and berated while the one (and usually it is only one) who is doing the wrong thing is totally oblivious of it. This type of movement tends to lead to a feeling among employees that they are going to be pounced on by spies lurking around every corner at any moment. Stress levels are high, morale is low, and people get tired of this and leave. This is no good for anyone at all. I would like to say that a contingent of concerned faculty members needs to confront the administration with this problem, but I am afraid it sounds like everybody would prefer not to see or talk to the administrators again. If you have a strong and cohesive faculty, you might want to try school district or union mediation with the administration and the trusted faculty representatives to try to rectify the situation. Unionized states have various other options as well. Otherwise, individually, you always have the option to get out of a bad situation and get another job. The second scenario seems to be the one most taken because it offers the least resistance. If you really like the school and your colleagues, it might be worth the effort to try confronting the administration as a group. You will be less likely to be individually targeted by them if you involve the district as well. Unfortunately, without being forcefully told to change by their own bosses, administrators such as these do not change their stripes too often. Good luck!

The administration at my school has totally unrealistic expectations. They expect me to teach using a variety of techniques, plan in typewritten form for each day, contact each parent at least once every 9 weeks (I have

155 students!), be on at least five active committees and the chair of at least one of them, help with evaluations of junior teachers, sponsor at least one active student club, and the list goes on and on! I am supposed to do all of this during my planning period, which they routinely take away from me because they are short on substitutes and I have to sub for other teachers. Is it OK to say "enough already" and stop doing some of this stuff? I have no life!

Yes, it is OK to say "enough." Schoolteachers always have more on their plates than most humans can deal with, but what you are describing sounds overly unrealistic. Are you the only one experiencing this overload? If so, then you need to have a talk with your principal and describe your situation and request relief or, if it is impossible, extra pay. Do not laugh; it is worth a shot! However, chances are good that you are not the only one being treated unfairly and that this is affecting most of the faculty. If so, then you need to establish a faculty forum that will articulate the concerns of the faculty members and send representatives to meet with the administration. If the administration is unresponsive after this, you may want to request school district or union mediation in this matter. In either situation, be sure that your representatives come armed with solutions to the problems they are stating. It is not enough to complain without offering sensible alternatives. When presented with a well thought-out plan of action, administrators only have to accept it instead of thinking it up themselves. Most folks tend to like the type of action that involves no work other than saying yes. They get to appease faculty members and be proactive in solving problems at their school. What could be better? This approach should solve the problems, but it is up to you to get everyone organized!

The administration at my school consists of three people who never set foot outside their offices. I doubt they know my name or what I teach, let alone how I teach! They do not even make an effort when it comes to observing us for evaluations. They wait until the last minute and then do not even stay for a whole class. I understand everyone is busy, but by behaving in this way, they do not have a clue about what is really going on at the school. Some of it really needs some administration! Is there anything I can do or should I just let the school fall apart and leave them to wonder why?

It is very difficult to tell your boss that he or she is not doing a good job. OK, it is impossible to do that. The impact you could probably have on this situation is only with regard to yourself. Invite your administration to come to your room whenever you are doing something special such as having students present projects or playing tournaments with your cooperative learning groups. If they do not come, keep inviting them by giving them descriptions of what you are doing that is noteworthy such as your students' acting out a story they read or presenting their oral reports. Either they will come eventually or they will have a memory of the fact that you are an innovative teacher who cares about her work and wants to share it with others. You can also volunteer to teach other teachers your special techniques at inservices or teacher's meetings at your school. This makes you visible to both your school and district administrations as well as establishes you as an authority among your colleagues, and this may actually help some teachers who would benefit from your ideas. As an authority, you may have a greater opportunity to affect change.

Relationships With Administrators

My principal is a really fun guy. I like to hang out with him and his wife after work and on weekends. Unfortunately, I am starting to get the cold shoulder at work from my colleagues. I do not feel I am doing anything wrong. Any opinions?

Whoops! Major *faux pas* here, as far as your colleagues go. This is really an unfortunate situation because, regardless of what educators say, there truly is an *us* versus *them* mentality, and the *them* is not the students, it is the administration. When you go over to the other side, so to speak, any goodies that may come your way professionally, such as nicer rooms, expedient delivery of materials, and so on, will be blamed on your friendship with the principal. Likewise, the principal will be accused of favoritism. The bad news is, although you are not doing anything wrong, the perceptions you are creating will harm you and the principal. My question is, however, how does everyone seem to know about your friendship? Are you bragging? If so, then be quiet! Unless someone is particularly close to a colleague at work, he or she could not begin to tell you who that colleague's friends are or what they do after school or on weekends. Keep your mouth shut about the friendship and request your principal to do the same, and maybe you both can continue with it. If it is too far gone already, you might seriously want to consider transferring to another school in your school district to avoid these unfortunate perceptions.

There is a teacher at my school who always gets what she wants: the best room, the best classes, materials,

you name it. I understand that she is a really good
teacher and has won a lot of awards, but let's face it, if
we all had every advantage like she does, we would all
win awards, too! Is there anything we can do in the
name of equity?

Put yourself in the position of the administration for a minute.
If you had an employee who truly excelled and was recognized constantly for her outstanding work, wouldn't you want
to do everything in your power to keep that employee happy?
Nevertheless, I understand your frustration because you want
some of the goodies, too! Try requesting in person materials,
rooms, classes, or whatever it is you want. Explain to your principal why you need these things to make your classes succeed,
and further explain your plans for instruction for bettering test
scores (this is always a winning reason), for improving retention,
or whatever it may be that is a valid issue for your school. (Be
sure these are real needs you have for the real reasons you state
or your reputation will be tarnished!) This type of discussion
gives you an opportunity to shine for your boss because he or
she will understand the thought that goes into your work and
the results you are trying to achieve as well as realize the depth
of the concern you have for your students. Before you leave this
meeting with your principal, make sure you put the paperwork
and requisitions in their hands and ask when you could expect
receipt of the goods. Follow up with a thank-you note to the
principal expressing gratitude for the time he or she spent talking with you and restate the agreed date of delivery of the goods
and services you want. If nothing happens by the time a week
has passed beyond the date you expected, request another meeting and discuss the problem. Most likely, the principal really did
try to answer your requests. There may be a bureaucratic snafu
somewhere that he or she could expedite for you. If you do all

this, it is highly unlikely that you will fail to receive what you truly need.

EVALUATIONS

୭ଓ

I believe I have been unfairly evaluated by administrators who would not know current teaching practices if it slapped them in the face. What recourse do I have?

୭ଓ

You need to check with your district, your union, or your state Department of Education's Office of Teacher Certification and Evaluation to identify the formal procedures for responding to an unfair evaluation. You may have the right to request another evaluation by different evaluators. However, you may be required to answer each charge in which you have a disagreement by providing a detailed explanation of your actions, hopefully supported by current teaching practice research. A lot depends on the level of contract you possess. A tenured teacher requires a great deal more than one unfavorable evaluation every 3 years to be fired. Newer teachers possess less legal rights, and these rights vary by state. Nevertheless, your professionalism has been called into question, and you have every right to be upset and defend yourself against an unfair, uninformed evaluation. If you are convinced of your correctness regarding your classroom behavior, follow all the prescribed bureaucratic channels to have your evaluation removed from your personnel file. It is possible that the administrator will voluntarily re-evaluate you if it is explained to him or her how you intend to go about reinstating your good professional standing as well as the fact that your teaching methods are supported by current teaching practice research. Not many administrators wish to appear uninformed by having their ignorance of new ways of teaching exposed. If all else fails, you might want to get legal advice from your union or educational association lawyer. Good luck!

> I really believe that the administrators at my school have not taught in 20 or 30 years. They come in my classroom expecting to see the classroom of the 1940s or 1950s, and the kids today are just different. Not to mention the fact that teachers are constantly being told to teach differently. How can I even begin to deal with these out-of-touch and out-of-date administrators?

These administrators are classic old-school administrators who have been trained in new teaching methodologies and attend all the workshops, but in their heads and hearts they are stuck in the mythical 1940s classroom full of bright shining faces eager to learn and a pin could be heard dropping at any point in an hour-long lecture. You need to bring them up to date. Explain to them what is happening in your classroom in terms of recent teaching methodologies. Say, for example,

> Hi, Mr. Smith, I'm so glad you stopped by today. You can observe my cooperative learning groups working on their open-ended tasks. I know you are interested in seeing this in action, as this is such an important teaching technique. I'm trying to incorporate rubrics into this activity to get the kids used to them, just like in that workshop we attended together. Please feel free to ask me any questions.

In fact, giving any visitor to your classroom a context in which to judge what they are seeing is helpful whether they are evaluating you or not. If they are doing a formal evaluation, you have actually helped them to write up their comments in advance by giving them the technical language for their report.

> I am in serious disagreement with the administration of my school about a situation that has arisen in one of my classes. I am afraid to continue to voice my opinion because I am scheduled to be evaluated this year, but my conscience will not let me be silent. What should I do?

A lot depends on the administration at your school. If they are reasonable people but just in disagreement with you then you are probably safe to continue to let your conscience speak. However, try to document everything. Do not let it be a situation where you rely only on verbal communication. You should send all your comments and concerns in writing and you should request that all responses be in writing as well. This will be a good idea, too, for an administration that is unreasonable. In fact, in this situation, it is especially important to keep all communication in writing. Furthermore, with unreasonable administrators, you may want to request mediation from the district or union if your disagreement is truly serious enough and you feel that it might jeopardize your evaluation. You will definitely want to have witnesses from outside of your school who can attest to the ongoing controversy in case your administration tries to retaliate. In any case, you have to live with yourself for a long time, and feeling strongly as you do about this situation, I fear you will regret not speaking your conscience and taking a stand. Just protect yourself from those who might try to harm you because of it.

My school uses peer observations as part of our evaluations. I am very uncomfortable with this because I do not
want my colleagues to see my problem areas. I would
rather they be kept between my administrator and myself.
Am I missing the point of these things or am I right to feel
this way?

You are missing the point of peer observations. Teachers are so
isolated from each other that it is a real treat to be able to
observe another teacher at work and learn from them. If you are
having a problem in a certain area, maybe one of your peers had
the same problem and has found a way to solve it. Wouldn't
you like to have that information? Everybody has problems
with their teaching; if they say otherwise, they are just pompous
teachers who think they know it all when in fact they are too
blind to their own faults. Besides, if there is a problem with your
teaching, you probably want to get it fixed via some help from
peers rather than have it laid before you as a glaring professional error during a formal evaluation by your administrator.
All of this is assuming that your department operates in a colle-
gial and friendly manner. If there is in-fighting and back-
stabbing going on as well as cliquish behavior, then you are right
to be concerned about peer observations and the ways in which
a peer who is unhappy with you could potentially hurt you professionally by unfair observations. If peer observations are
required, then there is usually a clause that allows you to reject
a peer as a member of your evaluation team because you feel
that person will not be fair to you. Investigate this and present
it to a sympathetic person who is in charge. Even if nothing is
done, you should have a written statement in your personnel
file that you requested removal of this peer from your evaluation team. This is just in case some injustice is done to you.

Sometimes I feel like I am being scammed by my administration, and even by my district, about what is and is not legal in the manner that they treat me. Is there some way to get a handle on the laws pertaining to my employment status without going to a lawyer? I believe I would feel more empowered sometimes if I just knew exactly what my rights were.

If you are in no hurry legally, you should register for a graduate level course at your local university or college in education law. Many times this course is taught by the department that deals with certification of administrators. It should give you an excellent overview of the laws affecting teachers and individual teacher rights. Courses that teach personnel management for the schools are also taught in educational administration departments and provide another good source of legal rights for the hiring, firing, and evaluation of teachers. Another source would be the Office of Teacher Certification and Evaluation in your state's Department of Education. They can answer questions dealing with contractual and certification issues. If you have a more pressing need for information and possible assistance, check with the professional groups you are affiliated with. They often have a legal aid department. If you are a member of a state or local union, obviously they have attorneys able to assist you with critical issues, and they may even offer short courses regarding your rights as well. Finally, there is nothing to beat the library, particularly law libraries. Often, law libraries have law students working there who can help you quickly locate the information you need because law libraries sometimes seem to be operating on an entirely different organizational scheme than regular libraries.

CHAPTER **8**
&

I Hope I Die During an Inservice So That the Transition Will Be Easy

Professional Development

Can there be anything in the world more frustrating than sitting through a 4-hour inservice on a topic of no use to you and presented in the most boring manner possible while you know you have 150 grades to average, 150 essays to grade, 14 parent calls to return, and 3 weeks of lesson plans to do? Ironically, much of the time the inservice topic is innovative alternatives to lecture, but it is presented in a lecture format that lasts all day! Before you become hysterical during one of these inevitable professional development endurance tests, take a deep breath and decide how you can work this situation to your advantage professionally and personally. In this chapter are some ideas on how you might accomplish this seemingly impossible challenge.

104

∞

I have yet another inservice coming up. Needless to say, I have a million other things to do at work that are more important. How can I survive one of these things again without being bored to tears and angry about such a waste of time?

∞

This is the fly in the oatmeal for most teachers. At any given moment in an inservice, a teacher has 12 other things he or she should be doing. However, inservices are a fact of life. Sometimes they are interesting and useful, and sometimes they are not. So do what you tell your students to do: Become an active participant. Ask questions (but not so many that you stop everyone from leaving for lunch or getting out early). Volunteer to help the presenter or be the guinea pig in his or her demonstrations. Surely there are one or two useful facts, so jot them down. Ask how you can apply this specifically to your classes. If none of this is working and you are truly stuck in the inservice from hell, then surely you have some lists to make, some problems for your class to figure out, lesson plans to design, or something inconspicuous that you need to do that will pass the time. Try not to be noticeable about it because there is no reason to hurt the presenter's feelings. This is not unprofessional. What is unprofessional is being made to spend your valuable time in an unproductive way. It is far better to try to get what you can out of one of these unfortunate inservices, and use the remainder of your time wisely.

∞

Other than recertification courses, is there really any reason to take advanced courses and go to workshops if they will not increase my salary, tenure, or standing at work?

The fact is, you should choose your workshops and advanced courses very carefully so that they will provide some advancement for you. For example, if you are somewhat interested in using technology in your classroom, arrange to take courses dealing with this topic. Not only will you learn something you are interested in but you will also soon become known as the expert in that particular field among your school faculty. Continue to increase your knowledge and you will find yourself becoming the expert in your district, your county, your state, and so on. Get the idea? You want to advance yourself, so like all professions, you need the knowledge that will enable you to get out there and promote your unique skills. Besides, the more you know, the better you can teach the students you have until that day when you become the guest educator on the *Today* show!

Why do I have to keep being recertified? This seems to be just another attack on the professionalism of teachers, as if we would not have enough sense on our own to keep current in our profession without being forced to do it!

It truly grieves me to say that there is a segment of our profession that gives all of us a bad name. These are teachers who are the classic bad educators: Those who do not know and do not want to know. Good teachers simply realize that recertification is a necessary part of being a teacher and use those courses to advance themselves and their knowledge in some way. Education is a political hot potato, and recertification is one way the politicians have of pointing to teachers and saying, "Look, we require them to keep current!" Besides, teaching is not the only profession that requires recertification periodically. Think about it this way: Would you want your doctor working on your health problems if the last time he or she had been in a medical training situation was 20 years ago? No! You want him or her to stay current, so why do you think your students and your students' parents want any less from you? To think otherwise really would be unprofessional.

Isn't there some other way to learn more and advance my knowledge than taking these endless classes and workshops?

You can join professional groups and become actively involved with them. Also, attend their seminars and conferences and network with other members. Surf the Internet and become an active member of chatrooms. I have known some teachers who became known as experts in particular areas just by participating in sites on the Web. These teachers were subsequently asked by universities and professional groups to be guest lecturers! Explore the larger educational market than that provided by your local university and your district. Education is big business and many companies specialize in training and materials for teachers in a wide array of areas. Volunteer for extracurricular activities and even extra duties at your school. You learn a lot about what really goes on behind the scenes at school and in so doing, you gain both knowledge and a reputation for being someone who is willing to go the extra mile. These may help you in your career immensely. You may also form networks of teachers at your school who observe each other with the idea of helping one another improve their teaching, observe a teacher who does something unique and try to use it in your classroom, or ask for professional leave time to observe excellent teachers at other schools. There is a lot of knowledge out there and lots of ways to get at it other than sitting in classes or workshops. Have fun!

The longer I teach, the more I feel that I am refining my interests in education to a few special areas such as technology and cooperative learning. Is this a good idea, or should I continue to be very broad in my scope of interest?

It is important to do both. Do not be so narrow that you suddenly realize that the boat has sailed into other areas of education and you were left behind. Always keep track of the big trends in education. The easiest way to do this is through regular reading of both a general educational journal as well as one in your field. However, read the previous question and answer regarding what you can do with your specific interests and abilities. Exploit and promote yourself! It is the way to get ahead in the business of education.

I feel that I have a lot of good ideas in the classroom that might benefit others. How can I best share my ideas?

Definitely do not hide your light under a bushel. This is how you get ahead in education: Make presentations of your great ideas. Volunteer at your district office to speak at inservices during the year for the entire district, or volunteer to give short demonstration lessons for other teachers in their classrooms or to give short lessons to the faculty members at your school during school meetings. Find your strong point—what you are really good at—and exploit it through presentations, articles in magazines, and even books! (Where do you think *this* book came from?) Once you have honed your presentation, hire yourself out to other districts during the summer for pay. You may even find you have yourself a new business!

∞

What are the best professional organizations to join?

∞

It is always good to be a member of both a state and national organization in your subject area. For example, I am a member of my state math teacher's association as well as the National Council of Teachers of Mathematics. It is also a good idea to be a member of a national organization that deals with administration or leadership, even if you are not interested in those areas, because they tend to dispense really good general educational information and tend to follow overall trends in education without being specific as to content. They give you a good overview of education. Finally, join one or two organizations that are specific to your interests such as curriculum development or educational research. All of these organizations will provide you with a well-rounded background, and their literature will help keep you current in a solid variety of educational arenas.

CHAPTER 9

QUESTION 100

Why Am I Doing This to Myself?

This chapter subtitle is an excellent question—one that you will ask yourself hundreds of times throughout your teaching career. On any given day, you are responsible for grading hundreds of papers, planning weeks of lessons, answering many telephone calls, contacting hundreds of parents, counseling many students, sponsoring clubs, advising on committees, instructing student teachers, holding lunch and other peripheral duties, copying tests, monitoring the behavior of hundreds of students, and actually trying to impart knowledge for 5 or more hours a day in an entertaining and motivating manner and still you are asked, "Why haven't you done [insert unreasonable request here]?" And you ask, "Why, why, why?"

You may deal with a variety of unsavory people each day: unreasonable administrators; irate and abusive parents; disrespectful and lazy students; young people who are drinking, smoking, fighting, having sex, cheating, lying, and so on and all on school grounds! You may witness fights, arrests, weapons, drug deals, sexual harassment, pregnant teenagers giving each other baby showers in the cafeteria, thefts, vandalism, and other things that most people rarely come into contact with on a daily basis. It begins to wear you down and you ask, "Why, why, why?"

Added to all of this, you read the newspaper that implies that teachers are the root cause for the declining intelligence of our youth and must be held accountable. Good teachers wonder what more they are supposed to do. We cannot open our students' heads and pour in the knowledge if they do not want to receive it! Holding teachers 100% accountable for student test scores is like holding doctors accountable when patients do not get well because they failed to take their medicine, or holding lawyers responsible when their clients go to jail because they failed to take their lawyer's advice. When parents and students and even administrators ask you, "Why is this student failing? What are you not doing for them?," you want to scream, "When are you going to hold the students accountable for their own learning?" Again you ask, "Why, why, why?"

Nobody understands the difficulty of what you do every day. All anyone can think about is how easy you have it because you have the summer off. They do not realize that most of us would go crazy if we had no relief from what we go through every day. They also do not realize that there are many days you would think it was pure heaven if all you had to do was push papers at a desk from 9 to 5, with a whole hour to yourself at lunch to go out and be an adult with other adults. Other people have no idea what it is like to perform on a stage for hundreds of students for 5 hours a day while monitoring and correcting their behavior. They do not understand that you do this many times while you have a fever of 101° because it is too hard to get a substitute. Why, why, why?

You have to answer the *why* for yourself. What keeps you going each day? Is it the light in the eyes when someone "gets it" after trying really hard? Is it the hugs and notes of thanks from students whose lives you have touched in some way? Is it the phone calls from parents just thanking you for being a good teacher and making a difference in their children's lives? Maybe it is the variety (how each day is different from the next), or maybe it is the fact that you have control over the direction your classes will take and the activities they will engage in. Perhaps you simply enjoy your subject and really like to let others know about it. Whatever it is that keeps you going every day, just remember that it really is worthwhile to be a teacher. If all you do is make a difference in a few young lives every year, at least you made a difference. Sometimes you are the only role model and the only guide these young people get. They need you whether they seem to or not and whether they know it or not.

Do not give up, and keep the faith. It really is worth it, you know.